# SPECTRUM®

# Multiplication

# Grade 4

Spectrum®
An imprint of Carson-Dellosa Publishing LLC
P.O. Box 35665
Greensboro, NC 27425  USA

ISBN 978-1-4838-0476-7

04-194151151

# Table of Contents Grade 4

*Spectrum Multiplication* is designed to build a solid foundation in multiplication for your fourth grader. Aligned to the fourth grade Common Core State Standards for multiplication, every page equips your child with the confidence to master multiplication. Helpful examples provide step-by-step guidance to teach new concepts, followed by a variety of practice pages that will sharpen your child's skills and efficiency at problem solving. Use the Pretests, Posttests, Mid-Test, and Final Test as the perfect way to track your child's progress and identify where he or she needs extra practice.

### **Common Core State Standards Alignment: Multiplication Grade 4**

| Domain: Operations and Algebraic Thinking | |
|---|---|
| Standard | Aligned Practice Pages |
| 4.OA.1 | 6, 11–13, 33 |
| 4.OA.2 | 35, 36, 45, 82 |
| 4.OA.3 | 32–43, 45, 64–76, 80–82 |
| 4.OA.5 | 10–13, 44–45, 79–80 |
| **Domain: Number and Operations in Base Ten** | |
| Standard | Aligned Practice Pages |
| 4.NBT.1 | 9, 14, 20, 24, 34, 47, 65 |
| 4.NBT.3 | 62, 74–76, 78, 80 |
| 4.NBT.5 | 5–82 |

# Check What You Know

## Multiplying through 4 Digits by 1 Digit

Multiply.

| | a | b | c | d | e |
|---|---|---|---|---|---|
| **1.** | 37<br>× 4 | 8<br>×3 | 75<br>× 2 | 6<br>×5 | 68<br>× 2 |
| **2.** | 76<br>× 2 | 359<br>× 4 | 34<br>× 6 | 638<br>× 5 | 48<br>× 2 |
| **3.** | 45<br>× 6 | 2467<br>× 3 | 43<br>× 4 | 5<br>×2 | 839<br>× 5 |
| **4.** | 64<br>× 3 | 83<br>× 6 | 45<br>× 3 | 4363<br>× 5 | 93<br>× 4 |
| **5.** | 6<br>×2 | 473<br>× 5 | 5966<br>× 4 | 25<br>× 6 | 4874<br>× 3 |
| **6.** | 923<br>× 6 | 97<br>× 2 | 447<br>× 5 | 77<br>× 4 | 84<br>× 4 |

# Understanding Multiplication

two times seven

2 × 7 means 7 + 7

|  |  |  |  |
|---|---|---|---|
| 7 | factor | | 7 |
| × 2 | factor | + | 7 |
| 1 4 | product | | 1 4 |

five times three

5 × 3 means 5 + 5 + 5

|  |  |  |  |
|---|---|---|---|
| | | | 5 |
| 5 | factor | | 5 |
| × 3 | factor | + | 5 |
| 1 5 | product | | 1 5 |

Multiply. Write the corresponding addition problem next to each multiplication problem.

|  | a | b | c | d | e |
|---|---|---|---|---|---|
| **1.** | 3  3 <br> ×2 +3 <br> ——  —— <br> 6   6 | 7 <br> ×2 <br> —— | 6 <br> ×2 <br> —— | 9 <br> ×2 <br> —— | 8 <br> ×2 <br> —— |
| **2.** | 2 <br> ×2 <br> —— | 1 <br> ×2 <br> —— | 5 <br> ×3 <br> —— | 6 <br> ×3 <br> —— | 3 <br> ×3 <br> —— |
| **3.** | 2 <br> ×3 <br> —— | 1 <br> ×3 <br> —— | 4 <br> ×3 <br> —— | 7 <br> ×3 <br> —— | 2 <br> ×4 <br> —— |
| **4.** | 4 <br> ×4 <br> —— | 1 <br> ×4 <br> —— | 5 <br> ×4 <br> —— | 9 <br> ×4 <br> —— | 8 <br> ×4 <br> —— |

# Multiplying Single Digits

factor $\longrightarrow$ 7 $\longrightarrow$ Find the **7**-column.

factor $\longrightarrow$ $\times$ 3 $\longrightarrow$ Find the **3**-row.

product $\longrightarrow$ 2 1 $\longrightarrow$ The product is named where the 7-column and the 3-row meet.

**7-column**

| x | 0 | 1 | 2 | 3 | 4 | 5 | 6 | 7 | 8 | 9 |
|---|---|---|---|---|---|---|---|---|---|---|
| 0 | 0 | 0 | 0 | 0 | 0 | 0 | 0 | 0 | 0 | 0 |
| 1 | 0 | 1 | 2 | 3 | 4 | 5 | 6 | 7 | 8 | 9 |
| 2 | 0 | 2 | 4 | 6 | 8 | 10 | 12 | 14 | 16 | 18 |
| 3 | 0 | 3 | 6 | 9 | 12 | 15 | 18 | 21 | 24 | 27 |
| 4 | 0 | 4 | 8 | 12 | 16 | 20 | 24 | 28 | 32 | 36 |
| 5 | 0 | 5 | 10 | 15 | 20 | 25 | 30 | 35 | 40 | 45 |
| 6 | 0 | 6 | 12 | 18 | 24 | 30 | 36 | 42 | 48 | 54 |
| 7 | 0 | 7 | 14 | 21 | 28 | 35 | 42 | 49 | 56 | 63 |
| 8 | 0 | 8 | 16 | 24 | 32 | 40 | 48 | 56 | 64 | 72 |
| 9 | 0 | 9 | 18 | 27 | 36 | 45 | 54 | 63 | 72 | 81 |

**3-row**

Use the table to multiply.

Multiply.

|  | a | b | c | d | e | f |
|---|---|---|---|---|---|---|
| **1.** | 3 ×3 | 8 ×7 | 2 ×9 | 7 ×5 | 9 ×4 | 6 ×6 |
| **2.** | 9 ×9 | 4 ×3 | 5 ×3 | 4 ×4 | 7 ×7 | 9 ×3 |
| **3.** | 8 ×5 | 6 ×4 | 8 ×2 | 9 ×7 | 4 ×8 | 7 ×3 |
| **4.** | 1 ×1 | 9 ×5 | 8 ×6 | 7 ×6 | 9 ×6 | 7 ×8 |

# Multiplying Single Digits

Fill in the missing number.

|  | a | b | c | d | e |
|---|---|---|---|---|---|
| **1.** | 6<br>× 9<br>□ | □<br>× 6<br>42 | 5<br>× □<br>25 | □<br>× 5<br>5 | 8<br>× □<br>72 |
| **2.** | 4<br>× □<br>16 | 2<br>× 4<br>□ | □<br>× 6<br>18 | 7<br>× 7<br>□ | □<br>× 2<br>6 |
| **3.** | □<br>× 7<br>56 | 8<br>× □<br>24 | 8<br>× 3<br>□ | 9<br>× □<br>63 | □<br>× 6<br>30 |
| **4.** | 3<br>× □<br>15 | 8<br>× 8<br>□ | 4<br>× □<br>32 | □<br>× 5<br>45 | 1<br>× □<br>8 |

# Multiplying 2 Digits by 1 Digit

$$
\begin{array}{r} 3\,2 \\ \times\ \ 3 \\ \hline 6 \end{array}
$$
Multiply 2 ones by 3.
$2 \times 3 = 6$

$$
\begin{array}{r} 3\,2 \\ \times\ \ 3 \\ \hline \underline{9}\,6 \end{array}
$$
Multiply 3 tens by 3.
$30 \times 3 = 90$

Multiply.

|     | **a** | **b** | **c** | **d** | **e** | **f** |
|-----|-------|-------|-------|-------|-------|-------|
| **1.** | $\begin{array}{r}23\\\times\ 2\\\hline\end{array}$ | $\begin{array}{r}71\\\times\ 1\\\hline\end{array}$ | $\begin{array}{r}12\\\times\ 4\\\hline\end{array}$ | $\begin{array}{r}33\\\times\ 2\\\hline\end{array}$ | $\begin{array}{r}10\\\times\ 7\\\hline\end{array}$ | $\begin{array}{r}24\\\times\ 2\\\hline\end{array}$ |
| **2.** | $\begin{array}{r}44\\\times\ 2\\\hline\end{array}$ | $\begin{array}{r}43\\\times\ 2\\\hline\end{array}$ | $\begin{array}{r}90\\\times\ 1\\\hline\end{array}$ | $\begin{array}{r}22\\\times\ 4\\\hline\end{array}$ | $\begin{array}{r}12\\\times\ 3\\\hline\end{array}$ | $\begin{array}{r}14\\\times\ 2\\\hline\end{array}$ |
| **3.** | $\begin{array}{r}11\\\times\ 9\\\hline\end{array}$ | $\begin{array}{r}75\\\times\ 1\\\hline\end{array}$ | $\begin{array}{r}11\\\times\ 6\\\hline\end{array}$ | $\begin{array}{r}30\\\times\ 3\\\hline\end{array}$ | $\begin{array}{r}10\\\times\ 4\\\hline\end{array}$ | $\begin{array}{r}42\\\times\ 2\\\hline\end{array}$ |
| **4.** | $\begin{array}{r}11\\\times\ 7\\\hline\end{array}$ | $\begin{array}{r}10\\\times\ 2\\\hline\end{array}$ | $\begin{array}{r}33\\\times\ 0\\\hline\end{array}$ | $\begin{array}{r}13\\\times\ 3\\\hline\end{array}$ | $\begin{array}{r}20\\\times\ 3\\\hline\end{array}$ | $\begin{array}{r}31\\\times\ 2\\\hline\end{array}$ |

# Multiplication Practice

Multiply.

|  | a | b | c | d | e | f |
|---|---|---|---|---|---|---|
| 1. | 10 ×2 | 41 ×2 | 13 ×2 | 40 ×2 | 30 ×2 | 11 ×5 |
| 2. | 30 ×1 | 11 ×7 | 25 ×1 | 42 ×0 | 22 ×3 | 10 ×1 |
| 3. | 14 ×0 | 10 ×5 | 31 ×3 | 12 ×3 | 20 ×4 | 10 ×7 |

Find the rule and complete each table.

a

4.

| In | Out |
|---|---|
| 2 | 11 |
| 3 |  |
| 4 |  |
| 5 | 26 |
| 6 |  |

b

| In | Out |
|---|---|
| 1 |  |
| 3 | 25 |
| 5 | 43 |
| 7 |  |
| 9 |  |

c

| In | Out |
|---|---|
| 2 |  |
| 4 |  |
| 5 | 36 |
| 7 |  |
| 9 | 60 |

_____

# Multiplication Practice

Fill in the missing number.

|   | a | b | c | d | e |
|---|---|---|---|---|---|

**1.**

a.
```
    9
  × 6
  ────
  [ ]
```

b.
```
  [ ]
  × 7
  ────
   63
```

c.
```
    4
  ×[ ]
  ────
    4
```

d.
```
  [ ]
  × 8
  ────
   32
```

e.
```
  [ ]
  × 3
  ────
   12
```

**2.**

a.
```
    5
  × 6
  ────
  [ ]
```

b.
```
    4
  ×[ ]
  ────
   20
```

c.
```
    4
  ×[ ]
  ────
   40
```

d.
```
    4
  ×[ ]
  ────
   36
```

e.
```
    8
  × 8
  ────
  [ ]
```

**3.**

a.
```
    4
  ×[ ]
  ────
   28
```

b.
```
    7
  × 8
  ────
  [ ]
```

c.
```
    6
  ×[ ]
  ────
   42
```

d.
```
  [ ]
  × 9
  ────
   45
```

e.
```
  [ ]
  × 3
  ────
   21
```

Find the rule and complete each table.

**4.**

a.

| In | Out |
|----|-----|
| 3  |     |
| 5  | 24  |
| 6  |     |
| 9  |     |
| 10 | 44  |

_____

b.

| In | Out |
|----|-----|
| 4  | 25  |
| 6  | 39  |
| 8  |     |
| 11 |     |
| 12 |     |

_____

c.

| In | Out |
|----|-----|
| 1  |     |
| 7  |     |
| 8  | 62  |
| 10 |     |
| 11 | 86  |

_____

# Multiplication Practice

Fill in the missing number.

|  | **a** | **b** | **c** | **d** | **e** |
|---|---|---|---|---|---|

**1.**

a:
$$\begin{array}{r} 5 \\ \times\, 9 \\ \hline \square \end{array}$$

b:
$$\begin{array}{r} \square \\ \times\, 8 \\ \hline 16 \end{array}$$

c:
$$\begin{array}{r} \square \\ \times\, 2 \\ \hline 20 \end{array}$$

d:
$$\begin{array}{r} \square \\ \times\, 2 \\ \hline 6 \end{array}$$

e:
$$\begin{array}{r} 3 \\ \times\, 7 \\ \hline \square \end{array}$$

**2.**

a:
$$\begin{array}{r} 7 \\ \times\, \square \\ \hline 77 \end{array}$$

b:
$$\begin{array}{r} \square \\ \times\, 11 \\ \hline 55 \end{array}$$

c:
$$\begin{array}{r} 5 \\ \times\, 5 \\ \hline \square \end{array}$$

d:
$$\begin{array}{r} 9 \\ \times\, \square \\ \hline 9 \end{array}$$

e:
$$\begin{array}{r} 6 \\ \times\, \square \\ \hline 42 \end{array}$$

**3.**

a:
$$\begin{array}{r} 9 \\ \times\, \square \\ \hline 45 \end{array}$$

b:
$$\begin{array}{r} 10 \\ \times\, 8 \\ \hline \square \end{array}$$

c:
$$\begin{array}{r} 5 \\ \times\, 7 \\ \hline \square \end{array}$$

d:
$$\begin{array}{r} \square \\ \times\, 10 \\ \hline 20 \end{array}$$

e:
$$\begin{array}{r} \square \\ \times\, 3 \\ \hline 15 \end{array}$$

Find the rule and complete each table.

**4.**

**a**

| In | Out |
|---|---|
| 0 | |
| 3 | 16 |
| 5 | |
| 7 | 24 |
| 9 | |

**b**

| In | Out |
|---|---|
| 2 | 12 |
| 5 | |
| 8 | |
| 10 | |
| 12 | 42 |

**c**

| In | Out |
|---|---|
| 5 | |
| 6 | |
| 7 | 55 |
| 8 | 63 |
| 9 | |

_____ _____ _____

# Multiplication Practice

Fill in the missing number.

|     | a | b | c | d | e |
|-----|---|---|---|---|---|

**1.**

a
```
    9
×  1 1
─────
  ☐
```

b
```
   ☐
×  2
────
  24
```

c
```
  ☐
×  4
────
  28
```

d
```
  1 0
×   7
─────
  ☐
```

e
```
  1 0
×  ☐
─────
  20
```

**2.**

a
```
   4
×  ☐
────
  20
```

b
```
  ☐
×  6
────
  36
```

c
```
   8
×  ☐
────
  48
```

d
```
  1 2
×   4
─────
  ☐
```

e
```
   2
×  ☐
────
  20
```

**3.**

a
```
  ☐
×  3
────
  12
```

b
```
  ☐
×  1 2
─────
  72
```

c
```
  1 1
×  ☐
─────
  77
```

d
```
   3
×  9
────
  ☐
```

e
```
   9
×  ☐
────
  81
```

Find the rule and complete each table.

|   | a |   |
|---|---|---|

**4.**

a

| In | Out |
|----|-----|
| 1  | 5   |
| 5  |     |
| 7  |     |
| 9  | 77  |
| 10 |     |

b

| In | Out |
|----|-----|
| 2  |     |
| 3  |     |
| 4  |     |
| 5  | 7   |
| 6  | 9   |

c

| In | Out |
|----|-----|
| 0  |     |
| 1  |     |
| 4  | 21  |
| 6  |     |
| 8  | 37  |

_____        _____        _____

# Multiplying 2 Digits by 1 Digit

$\overset{1}{7}2$
$\times\ \ 8$
$\underline{\phantom{00}6}$ ← Put 6 under the ones place.
    Add the 10 above the 7.

Multiply 2 ones by 8.
    $2 \times 8 = 16$ or $10 + 6$

$\overset{1}{7}2$
$\times\ \ \ 8$
$\underline{5\,7\,6}$

Multiply 7 tens by 8.
    Then, add 1 ten.
$70 \times 8 = 560 \rightarrow 560 + 10 =$
    $570$ or $500 + 70$

Multiply.

|   | a | b | c | d | e | f |
|---|---|---|---|---|---|---|
| 1. | 73<br>× 4 | 25<br>× 2 | 36<br>× 3 | 52<br>× 5 | 23<br>× 4 | 42<br>× 5 |
| 2. | 19<br>× 2 | 26<br>× 2 | 68<br>× 3 | 54<br>× 5 | 47<br>× 8 | 33<br>× 4 |
| 3. | 32<br>× 9 | 48<br>× 8 | 52<br>× 3 | 34<br>× 4 | 17<br>× 5 | 22<br>× 5 |
| 4. | 66<br>× 3 | 45<br>× 5 | 66<br>× 5 | 19<br>× 9 | 38<br>× 9 | 74<br>× 3 |

# Multiplying 2 Digits by 1 Digit

Multiply.

|  | a | b | c | d | e | f |
|---|---|---|---|---|---|---|
| 1. | 55<br>× 3 | 64<br>× 8 | 83<br>× 5 | 49<br>× 7 | 50<br>× 9 | 86<br>× 6 |
| 2. | 60<br>× 6 | 17<br>× 3 | 48<br>× 9 | 75<br>× 3 | 60<br>× 9 | 96<br>× 5 |
| 3. | 31<br>× 9 | 77<br>× 4 | 82<br>× 3 | 96<br>× 3 | 40<br>× 7 | 79<br>× 2 |
| 4. | 42<br>× 6 | 19<br>× 5 | 83<br>× 3 | 16<br>× 6 | 14<br>× 8 | 91<br>× 4 |

# Multiplication Practice

Multiply.

|  | a | b | c | d | e | f |
|---|---|---|---|---|---|---|
| 1. | 13<br>× 5 | 38<br>× 2 | 14<br>× 8 | 15<br>× 6 | 36<br>× 3 | 39<br>× 2 |
| 2. | 27<br>× 4 | 28<br>× 3 | 47<br>× 2 | 16<br>× 9 | 15<br>× 5 | 13<br>× 7 |
| 3. | 17<br>× 6 | 25<br>× 4 | 24<br>× 3 | 45<br>× 2 | 16<br>× 8 | 14<br>× 7 |
| 4. | 29<br>× 2 | 16<br>× 4 | 37<br>× 3 | 16<br>× 5 | 48<br>× 2 | 19<br>× 4 |

# Multiplication Practice

Multiply.

|     | a | b | c | d | e | f |
|-----|------|------|------|------|------|------|
| **1.** | 26<br>× 3 | 64<br>× 5 | 43<br>× 8 | 57<br>× 6 | 98<br>× 2 | 35<br>× 4 |
| **2.** | 76<br>× 3 | 46<br>× 7 | 85<br>× 3 | 35<br>× 8 | 23<br>× 9 | 62<br>× 5 |
| **3.** | 42<br>× 6 | 73<br>× 4 | 82<br>× 5 | 67<br>× 3 | 27<br>× 8 | 49<br>× 7 |
| **4.** | 88<br>× 2 | 36<br>× 9 | 53<br>× 6 | 83<br>× 4 | 65<br>× 5 | 34<br>× 8 |

# Multiplication Practice

Multiply.

|  | a | b | c | d | e | f |
|---|---|---|---|---|---|---|
| 1. | 84<br>× 5 | 35<br>× 7 | 63<br>× 8 | 57<br>× 4 | 55<br>× 9 | 43<br>× 6 |
| 2. | 92<br>× 8 | 42<br>× 9 | 85<br>× 6 | 53<br>× 4 | 74<br>× 8 | 83<br>× 5 |
| 3. | 65<br>× 7 | 87<br>× 3 | 49<br>× 6 | 23<br>× 9 | 86<br>× 4 | 35<br>× 8 |
| 4. | 82<br>× 5 | 32<br>× 9 | 46<br>× 6 | 89<br>× 2 | 64<br>× 7 | 43<br>× 9 |

**SCORE** ⬭ **/ 24**

## Multiplication Practice

Multiply.

|  | a | b | c | d | e | f |
|---|---|---|---|---|---|---|
| 1. | 76 ×4 | 23 ×6 | 49 ×8 | 64 ×5 | 87 ×9 | 43 ×7 |
| 2. | 88 ×3 | 73 ×6 | 54 ×8 | 69 ×5 | 74 ×9 | 39 ×7 |
| 3. | 83 ×9 | 45 ×6 | 75 ×8 | 62 ×7 | 28 ×9 | 52 ×8 |
| 4. | 63 ×5 | 77 ×3 | 38 ×9 | 97 ×2 | 48 ×7 | 53 ×9 |

# Multiplying 3 Digits by 1 Digit

$$\begin{array}{r} \overset{1}{7}52 \\ \times\quad 8 \\ \hline 6 \end{array}$$ Multiply 2 ones by 8.
Put 1 ten above the 5.

$$\begin{array}{r} \overset{4\ 1}{7}52 \\ \times\quad 8 \\ \hline \underline{1}6 \end{array}$$ Multiply 5 tens by 8. Then, add 1 ten.
Put 4 hundreds above the 7.

$$\begin{array}{r} \overset{4\ 1}{7}52 \\ \times\quad 8 \\ \hline 60\underline{1}6 \end{array}$$ Multiply 7 hundreds by 8.
Then, add 4 hundreds.

---

Multiply.

|  | **a** | **b** | **c** | **d** | **e** |
|---|---|---|---|---|---|
| **1.** | 118 ×3 | 305 ×4 | 224 ×5 | 152 ×3 | 200 ×7 |
| **2.** | 327 ×3 | 158 ×3 | 235 ×6 | 142 ×9 | 580 ×3 |
| **3.** | 335 ×5 | 190 ×7 | 421 ×8 | 201 ×9 | 287 ×3 |
| **4.** | 405 ×5 | 118 ×8 | 402 ×3 | 498 ×6 | 700 ×7 |

# Multiplying 3 Digits by 1 Digit

Multiply.

|  | a | b | c | d | e |
|---|---|---|---|---|---|
| **1.** | 137<br>× 5 | 129<br>× 9 | 243<br>× 4 | 398<br>× 2 | 652<br>× 3 |
| **2.** | 142<br>× 4 | 704<br>× 8 | 193<br>× 7 | 246<br>× 3 | 152<br>× 7 |
| **3.** | 704<br>× 6 | 751<br>× 3 | 200<br>× 7 | 555<br>× 2 | 909<br>× 2 |
| **4.** | 730<br>× 7 | 328<br>× 7 | 462<br>× 6 | 294<br>× 3 | 847<br>× 4 |

**SCORE** ⬭ **/ 25**

# Multiplication Practice

Multiply.

|  | a | b | c | d | e |
|---|---|---|---|---|---|
| 1. | 416<br>× 4 | 318<br>× 6 | 379<br>× 2 | 719<br>× 9 | 168<br>× 7 |
| 2. | 713<br>× 8 | 219<br>× 6 | 237<br>× 5 | 279<br>× 3 | 173<br>× 9 |
| 3. | 164<br>× 6 | 179<br>× 8 | 716<br>× 7 | 298<br>× 4 | 836<br>× 3 |
| 4. | 632<br>× 5 | 218<br>× 9 | 816<br>× 8 | 421<br>× 6 | 248<br>× 2 |
| 5. | 541<br>× 7 | 918<br>× 4 | 641<br>× 9 | 836<br>× 3 | 941<br>× 8 |

## Multiplication Practice

Multiply.

|  | a | b | c | d | e |
|---|---|---|---|---|---|
| 1. | 423<br>× 6 | 735<br>× 3 | 817<br>× 9 | 325<br>× 5 | 316<br>× 8 |
| 2. | 326<br>× 6 | 623<br>× 4 | 231<br>× 7 | 687<br>× 3 | 823<br>× 4 |
| 3. | 912<br>× 9 | 813<br>× 6 | 912<br>× 8 | 867<br>× 2 | 613<br>× 7 |
| 4. | 524<br>× 5 | 716<br>× 6 | 532<br>× 5 | 921<br>× 8 | 703<br>× 4 |
| 5. | 608<br>× 9 | 517<br>× 7 | 123<br>× 9 | 312<br>× 7 | 768<br>× 2 |

# Multiplying 4 Digits by 1 Digit

Multiply from right to left.

$2 \times 7 = 14 + 2 = ⑯$
$3 \times 7 = 21 + 1 = 22$

$\begin{array}{r} \overset{1\ 2\ 4}{3236} \\ \times \qquad 7 \\ \hline 22652 \end{array}$

$6 \times 7 = ㊷$
$3 \times 7 = 21 + 4 = ㉕$

---

Multiply.

|   | a | b | c | d | e |
|---|---|---|---|---|---|
| **1.** | $\begin{array}{r} 2763 \\ \times \quad 5 \\ \hline \end{array}$ | $\begin{array}{r} 6204 \\ \times \quad 7 \\ \hline \end{array}$ | $\begin{array}{r} 3221 \\ \times \quad 4 \\ \hline \end{array}$ | $\begin{array}{r} 8634 \\ \times \quad 8 \\ \hline \end{array}$ | $\begin{array}{r} 7253 \\ \times \quad 6 \\ \hline \end{array}$ |
| **2.** | $\begin{array}{r} 4728 \\ \times \quad 4 \\ \hline \end{array}$ | $\begin{array}{r} 3962 \\ \times \quad 9 \\ \hline \end{array}$ | $\begin{array}{r} 1854 \\ \times \quad 2 \\ \hline \end{array}$ | $\begin{array}{r} 5273 \\ \times \quad 6 \\ \hline \end{array}$ | $\begin{array}{r} 4456 \\ \times \quad 3 \\ \hline \end{array}$ |
| **3.** | $\begin{array}{r} 7526 \\ \times \quad 3 \\ \hline \end{array}$ | $\begin{array}{r} 9428 \\ \times \quad 2 \\ \hline \end{array}$ | $\begin{array}{r} 3725 \\ \times \quad 8 \\ \hline \end{array}$ | $\begin{array}{r} 6414 \\ \times \quad 7 \\ \hline \end{array}$ | $\begin{array}{r} 2889 \\ \times \quad 4 \\ \hline \end{array}$ |
| **4.** | $\begin{array}{r} 5297 \\ \times \quad 6 \\ \hline \end{array}$ | $\begin{array}{r} 4175 \\ \times \quad 3 \\ \hline \end{array}$ | $\begin{array}{r} 8052 \\ \times \quad 4 \\ \hline \end{array}$ | $\begin{array}{r} 2988 \\ \times \quad 8 \\ \hline \end{array}$ | $\begin{array}{r} 6364 \\ \times \quad 2 \\ \hline \end{array}$ |

# Multiplying 4 Digits by 1 Digit

Multiply.

|  | a | b | c | d | e |
|---|---|---|---|---|---|
| **1.** | 2684<br>× 3 | 9436<br>× 7 | 8146<br>× 5 | 8938<br>× 2 | 5437<br>× 6 |
| **2.** | 8346<br>× 4 | 9136<br>× 3 | 8324<br>× 9 | 5324<br>× 3 | 2645<br>× 7 |
| **3.** | 9845<br>× 2 | 3247<br>× 6 | 6205<br>× 8 | 3879<br>× 4 | 4275<br>× 6 |
| **4.** | 6248<br>× 3 | 4189<br>× 5 | 7648<br>× 2 | 8154<br>× 7 | 3264<br>× 8 |

# Multiplication Practice

Multiply.

|  | a | b | c | d | e |
|---|---|---|---|---|---|
| **1.** | 6140<br>× 5 | 5389<br>× 2 | 6528<br>× 8 | 9476<br>× 3 | 4326<br>× 7 |
| **2.** | 7342<br>× 4 | 9465<br>× 6 | 3186<br>× 9 | 8547<br>× 5 | 2894<br>× 3 |
| **3.** | 2315<br>× 8 | 9478<br>× 2 | 3272<br>× 6 | 8675<br>× 4 | 4639<br>× 8 |
| **4.** | 9576<br>× 3 | 8964<br>× 5 | 9210<br>× 7 | 3948<br>× 6 | 8674<br>× 2 |
| **5.** | 5782<br>× 4 | 3546<br>× 9 | 3765<br>× 8 | 4268<br>× 3 | 7286<br>× 5 |

## Multiplication Practice

Multiply.

|  | a | b | c | d |
|---|---|---|---|---|
| **1.** | 48<br>× 7 | 64<br>× 3 | 235<br>× 5 | 829<br>× 8 |
| **2.** | 3146<br>× 2 | 7402<br>× 3 | 21<br>× 5 | 72<br>× 4 |
| **3.** | 49<br>× 5 | 380<br>× 2 | 816<br>× 2 | 276<br>× 8 |
| **4.** | 2714<br>× 5 | 5216<br>× 6 | 177<br>× 4 | 818<br>× 3 |
| **5.** | 445<br>× 6 | 3420<br>× 4 | 5867<br>× 2 | 6334<br>× 7 |

# Multiplication Practice

Multiply.

|  | a | b | c | d | e |
|---|---|---|---|---|---|
| 1. | 649 × 8 | 858 × 7 | 7642 × 5 | 8219 × 3 | 5238 × 6 |
| 2. | 4623 × 9 | 8249 × 4 | 6518 × 7 | 8943 × 9 | 3268 × 5 |
| 3. | 4637 × 8 | 8924 × 6 | 5387 × 4 | 8264 × 9 | 4875 × 7 |
| 4. | 5689 × 8 | 9243 × 4 | 7643 × 9 | 8540 × 6 | 3726 × 5 |

# Multiplication Practice

Multiply.

| a | b | c | d | e |
|---|---|---|---|---|

**1.**
$$3243 \times 6$$  $$4254 \times 7$$  $$2435 \times 9$$  $$5201 \times 5$$  $$3643 \times 8$$

**2.**
$$1476 \times 4$$  $$3629 \times 5$$  $$7642 \times 7$$  $$5624 \times 4$$  $$3928 \times 8$$

**3.**
$$8215 \times 6$$  $$1826 \times 9$$  $$3214 \times 8$$  $$3265 \times 4$$  $$5429 \times 5$$

**4.**
$$9267 \times 3$$  $$6254 \times 7$$  $$1242 \times 8$$  $$3263 \times 6$$  $$5584 \times 2$$

# Multiplication Practice

Multiply.

|  | a | b | c | d | e |
|---|---|---|---|---|---|
| **1.** | 6<br>×3 | 8<br>×2 | 4<br>×7 | 22<br>× 9 | 17<br>× 6 |
| **2.** | 74<br>× 6 | 34<br>× 9 | 28<br>× 6 | 163<br>× 1 | 317<br>× 4 |
| **3.** | 836<br>× 4 | 627<br>× 8 | 352<br>× 2 | 73<br>× 7 | 65<br>× 9 |
| **4.** | 26<br>× 5 | 84<br>× 8 | 92<br>× 3 | 258<br>× 4 | 736<br>× 8 |

# Check What You Learned

## Multiplying through 4 Digits by 1 Digit

Multiply.

|  | a | b | c | d | e |
|---|---|---|---|---|---|
| 1. | 26 <br> × 3 | 24 <br> × 4 | 647 <br> × 2 | 14 <br> × 6 | 9353 <br> × 4 |
| 2. | 739 <br> × 2 | 4 <br> ×7 | 25 <br> × 3 | 5613 <br> × 5 | 37 <br> × 2 |
| 3. | 48 <br> × 2 | 4623 <br> × 4 | 935 <br> × 2 | 12 <br> × 8 | 1324 <br> × 3 |
| 4. | 9413 <br> × 6 | 818 <br> × 5 | 29 <br> × 3 | 7 <br> ×5 | 49 <br> × 2 |
| 5. | 6 <br> ×6 | 36 <br> × 2 | 2818 <br> × 3 | 415 <br> × 6 | 27 <br> × 3 |
| 6. | 213 <br> × 7 | 28 <br> × 3 | 9 <br> ×5 | 46 <br> × 2 | 816 <br> × 5 |

**NAME** _____

# Check What You Know

## Problem Solving: Multiplying through 4 Digits by 1 Digit

Read the problem carefully and solve. Show your work under each question.

Sue's Supply Shop places an order for more office supplies. Sue orders 9 boxes of blue pens. Thirty-five pens come in each box. Paperclips come in boxes of 1,165, and she orders 7 boxes. She also orders 8 boxes of rulers, and 15 rulers come in each box.

1. Sue plans to have a sale on blue pens. How many blue pens does Sue order in total?


    _____ blue pens


2. How many total paperclips does Sue order?


    _____ paperclips


3. Sue wants to make sure she has enough space on her shelves for all the rulers she orders. How many rulers altogether does she order?


    _____ rulers


4. When Sue receives the order, she finds that 5 of the 9 pen boxes are filled with black pens instead of blue pens. How many blue pens does Sue have from the order?


    _____ blue pens

# Multiplying Single Digits

Read the problem carefully and solve. Show your work under each question.

Ella makes necklaces for a craft fair. For each necklace, she uses 4 yellow beads, 7 blue beads, 6 red beads, and 8 green beads.

> **Helpful Hint**
>
> To solve a multiplication word problem, you need to find:
>
> 1. the number of groups
> 2. the number of items in each group

**1.** Ella makes 9 necklaces. How many green beads does she use?

_____ green beads

**2.** How many yellow beads does Ella use to make 9 necklaces?

_____ yellow beads

**3.** To make 6 necklaces, how many red beads does Ella use? Write the corresponding addition problem.

_____ red beads

**SCORE ⬤ / 3**

# Multiplying 2 Digits by 1 Digit

Read the problem carefully and solve. Show your work under each question.

Roger and his friend Aaron like to go mountain biking. They keep track of the total miles they bike each week. Roger bikes 32 miles each week. Aaron bikes 23 miles each week.

**Helpful Hint**

To find the answer or product:

1. Multiply 3 ones by 2.

2. Then, multiply 2 tens by 2.

```
  2 3
× 2
─────
  4 6
```

**1.** After 3 weeks, how many miles has Roger biked in total?

_____ miles

**2.** Aaron calculates the total number of miles he biked in 3 weeks. How many miles did he bike?

_____ miles

**3.** Roger biked an extra mile each week for 3 weeks. How many total miles did he bike during those 3 weeks?

_____ miles

**SCORE** ◯ / 4

# Multiplying 2 Digits by 1 Digit

Solve each problem. Show your work under each question.

> **Helpful Hint**
>
> If you know the total number of items in a group and the number of groups, then you can write an equation to help you solve the problem using multiplication:
>
> $8 \times a = 96$
>
> $8 \times 12 = 96$
>
> $a = 12$

1. There are 48 chicken farms near an Ohio town. If each farm has 9 barns, how many total barns are there?

   There are _____ total barns.

2. Mr. Ferris has a canoe rental business. Over the weekend, he rented 47 canoes. A canoe holds 3 people. If each canoe was full, how many people did Mr. Ferris rent to over the weekend?

   Mr. Ferris rented to _____ people.

3. The school bought 368 slices of pizza to serve at the school dance. If the school planned for each student to have 4 slices of pizza, how many students will attend the dance? Write a multiplication equation to find how many students will attend the dance. Then, solve.

   _____          _____ students will attend the dance.

# Multiplying 2 Digits by 1 Digit

Solve each problem. Show your work under each question.

**1.** The pool opened on Memorial Day. Ninety-four people showed up. The pool manager gave out 2 vouchers to each person for free drinks. How many vouchers did the pool manager give out?

The manager gave out _____ vouchers.

**2.** In the Sumton community, there are 56 houses. If there are 3 children living in each house, how many children live in houses in Sumton?

There are _____ children living in houses in Sumton.

**3.** Deon and Denise need 115 dollars to buy a computer game. If they save the same amount of money each week for 5 weeks, how much money will they need to save each week? Write a multiplication equation to find how much Deon and Denise need to save each week. Then, solve.

_____          _____ dollars

# Multiplying 2 Digits by 1 Digit

Solve each problem. Show your work under each question.

1. Mr. Benson must order 32 calculators for each fifth grade class. There are 6 classes. How many calculators must Mr. Benson order?

   Each class needs _____ calculators.

   There are _____ classes.

   Mr. Benson must order _____ calculators.

2. It takes Rosa 73 minutes to knit a scarf. How many minutes will it take her to knit 4 scarves?

   It will take Rosa _____ minutes to knit a scarf.

   She wants to knit _____ scarves.

   It will take Rosa _____ minutes.

# Multiplying 3 Digits by 1 Digit

Read the problem carefully and solve. Show your work under each question.

A computer game company held a contest on Saturday. The company kept track of how many hours each person participated in the contest. 327 people played for 2 hours. 113 people played for 3 hours. 373 people played for 4 hours. 235 people played for 5 hours. 118 people played for 6 hours.

**Helpful Hint**

To find the total time a group of people spends on an activity, multiply the number of people by the time each one spends on the activity.

1. Which group of people played the most number of hours? How many total hours did they play?

   the group of _____ people

   _____ hours

2. Some of the participants played in the contest for 6 hours. How many total hours did these participants play?

   _____ hours

# Multiplying 3 Digits by 1 Digit

**3.** How many total hours did the group with 113 participants play in the contest?

_____ hours

**4.** One group of participants played for the shortest amount of time. How many total hours did this group play?

_____ hours

**5.** How many total hours did the group with 235 participants play in the contest?

_____ hours

# Multiplying 4 Digits by 1 Digit

Read the problem carefully and solve. Show your work under each question.

Jerome loves to help take care of the crops on his grandfather's farm. There are 8 rows of tomato plants with 1,209 plants in each row. The carrots are planted in 9 rows with 47 plants in each row. There are also 7 rows of pepper plants with 106 plants in each row.

---

**Helpful Hint**

When multiplying a number with zeros in it, remember to multiply and rename the places correctly:

$$\begin{array}{r} 2\overset{3}{0}8 \\ \times\phantom{00}4 \\ \hline 832 \end{array}$$

---

1. How many pepper plants are there in all? How many carrot plants are there in all?

   _____ pepper plants

   _____ carrot plants

2. Jerome loves tomatoes. What is the total number of tomato plants at the farm?

   _____ tomato plants

3. Jerome's grandfather wants to add 3 more rows of pepper plants. What is the total number of pepper plants he will add to his crop?

   _____ pepper plants

# Multiplication Practice

Solve each problem. Show your work under each question.

**1.** Tyrone practices baseball 2 hours a day, 4 days a week. How many hours does Tyrone practice baseball each week?

Tyrone practices _____ hours each week.

**2.** Alfonso studied for his science test 3 hours a day for 22 days. How many hours did Alfonzo study in all?

Alfonzo studied for _____ hours.

**3.** The symphony has 8 performances scheduled this year. There are 527 tickets available for each performance. If all the seats are filled for each performance, how many tickets will the symphony have sold?

The symphony will have sold _____ tickets.

## Multiplication Practice

Solve each problem. Show your work under each question.

1. Century High School is having a bake sale for the community. Each person is required to bring in 2 baked goods. If there are 2,537 students enrolled in the school, how many baked goods will there be for sale?

There will be _____ baked goods for sale.

2. If a lemonade stand serves 7 customers a day, 210 days a year, how many customers will the lemonade stand serve in a year?

The lemonade stand will serve _____ customers in a year.

3. There are 1,483 students in Eden's school. If each student brings in 9 cans of soup for a food drive, how many cans of soup will the school donate?

The school will donate _____ cans of soup.

# Check What You Learned

## Problem Solving: Multiplying through 4 Digits by 1 Digit

Read the problem carefully and solve. Show your work under each question.

Meiko plans to build models of some of the buildings in her city. She needs to keep track of the total number of windows per floor and the number of floors for each building. She lists this information in the chart to the right.

| Building Name | Number of windows per floor | Number of floors |
|---|---|---|
| Ivy Tower | 145 | 8 |
| Jackson Building | 95 | 7 |
| Sky Tower | 178 | 9 |

**CHAPTER 2 POSTTEST**

1. Meiko plans to make the Jackson Building first. How many windows does it have in all?

   _____ windows

2. Meiko's favorite building is the Ivy Tower. How many windows does it have in all?

   _____ windows

3. Which building has the largest number of windows in all? How many windows does this building have?

   The _____ has the largest number of windows with

   _____ windows.

4. Meiko learns that the Ivy Tower is fixing the windows on the top 5 floors of the building. How many windows are not being fixed?

   _____ windows

## Mid-Test Chapters 1–2

Multiply.

|  | a | b | c | d | e |
|---|---|---|---|---|---|
| 1. | 73<br>× 3 | 56<br>× 8 | 77<br>× 5 | 96<br>× 4 | 25<br>× 9 |
| 2. | 273<br>× 6 | 312<br>× 5 | 278<br>× 7 | 428<br>× 4 | 122<br>× 5 |
| 3. | 763<br>× 8 | 693<br>× 6 | 578<br>× 4 | 989<br>× 3 | 853<br>× 3 |
| 4. | 1215<br>× 4 | 2138<br>× 6 | 3155<br>× 2 | 4068<br>× 5 | 2100<br>× 3 |
| 5. | 6125<br>× 2 | 7312<br>× 3 | 8484<br>× 5 | 3167<br>× 2 | 9319<br>× 3 |

Find the rule and complete each table.

a

| In | Out |
|---|---|
| 3 | |
| 4 | 26 |
| 5 | |
| 6 | 38 |
| 7 | |

b

| In | Out |
|---|---|
| 2 | 15 |
| 5 | |
| 6 | |
| 9 | 71 |
| 10 | |

c

| In | Out |
|---|---|
| 3 | |
| 7 | 52 |
| 8 | |
| 11 | 80 |
| 12 | |

6. _____    _____    _____

## Mid-Test Chapters 1–2

Solve each problem. Show your work under each question.

7. Mrs. Numkena's science class raised 105 tadpoles. Each student raised 3 tadpoles. How many students are in Mrs. Numkena's science class? Write a multiplication equation to find how many students are in her class. Then, solve.

_____        _____ students are in the class.

8. At Lakeside View, 15 apartment buildings were built. If there are 8 units to each apartment building, how many units are available?

There are _____ units available.

9. Kyle and his brother collect seashells each year they go to the beach. If Kyle and his brother collect 112 seashells each day for 4 days, how many seashells will they add to their collection?

Kyle and his brother will add _____ seashells to their collection.

10. There are 1,560 rooms in Beachside Hotel. Each room is designed to fit four guests. If each room is filled, how many guest are staying at Beachside Hotel?

There are _____ guests staying at Beachside Hotel.

11. What is the next number in this pattern? Explain your answer.
2, 5, 14, 41, 122

_____

_____

**NAME** _____

# Check What You Know

## Multiplying through 3 Digits by 2 Digits

Multiply.

|  | a | b | c | d | e | f |
|---|---|---|---|---|---|---|
| **1.** | 17 ×28 | 25 ×43 | 302 × 13 | 17 ×15 | 10 ×39 | 12 ×12 |
| **2.** | 315 × 47 | 92 ×19 | 91 ×52 | 32 ×33 | 54 ×67 | 93 ×38 |
| **3.** | 605 × 40 | 79 ×21 | 100 × 22 | 44 ×38 | 117 × 23 | 49 ×58 |
| **4.** | 50 ×23 | 10 ×10 | 94 ×62 | 75 ×25 | 11 ×11 | 72 ×13 |
| **5.** | 452 × 92 | 88 ×22 | 73 ×61 | 66 ×47 | 78 ×73 | 802 × 16 |
| **6.** | 72 ×21 | 33 ×70 | 68 ×88 | 109 × 42 | 618 × 47 | 500 × 30 |
| **7.** | 102 × 30 | 44 ×18 | 891 × 29 | 792 × 36 | 107 × 5 | 19 ×13 |
| **8.** | 618 × 12 | 748 × 25 | 89 ×60 | 72 ×45 | 118 × 37 | 500 × 90 |

# Multiplying 2 Digits by 2 Digits

Multiply 9 ones by 7.

$$\begin{array}{r} 19 \\ \times 27 \\ \hline \end{array} \qquad \overset{6}{\underset{}{\begin{array}{r} 19 \\ \times 27 \\ \hline 133 \end{array}}}$$

Put 6 tens above the 1.
Multiply 1 ten by 7.
Then, add 6 tens.

$$\overset{1}{\underset{}{\begin{array}{r} 19 \\ \times 27 \\ \hline 133 \\ 38 \end{array}}}$$

Multiply 9 ones by 2.

Put 1 ten above the 1.
Multiply 1 ten by 2.
Then, add 1 ten.

$$\left.\begin{array}{r} 19 \\ \times\ 27 \\ \hline 133 \\ +380 \\ \hline 513 \end{array}\right\} \text{Add.}$$

Multiply.

|  | a | b | c | d | e | f |
|---|---|---|---|---|---|---|
| 1. | 22 ×33 | 11 ×45 | 80 ×10 | 31 ×23 | 13 ×12 | 30 ×31 |
| 2. | 41 ×21 | 32 ×20 | 40 ×10 | 21 ×31 | 30 ×30 | 14 ×10 |
| 3. | 22 ×44 | 14 ×20 | 40 ×12 | 90 ×10 | 13 ×13 | 30 ×11 |

# Multiplying 2 Digits by 2 Digits

Multiply.

|   | a | b | c | d | e | f |
|---|---|---|---|---|---|---|
| **1.** | $\begin{array}{r} 22 \\ \times 19 \\ \hline \end{array}$ | $\begin{array}{r} 32 \\ \times 41 \\ \hline \end{array}$ | $\begin{array}{r} 72 \\ \times 18 \\ \hline \end{array}$ | $\begin{array}{r} 45 \\ \times 15 \\ \hline \end{array}$ | $\begin{array}{r} 48 \\ \times 20 \\ \hline \end{array}$ | $\begin{array}{r} 77 \\ \times 22 \\ \hline \end{array}$ |
| **2.** | $\begin{array}{r} 63 \\ \times 24 \\ \hline \end{array}$ | $\begin{array}{r} 52 \\ \times 48 \\ \hline \end{array}$ | $\begin{array}{r} 28 \\ \times 25 \\ \hline \end{array}$ | $\begin{array}{r} 77 \\ \times 30 \\ \hline \end{array}$ | $\begin{array}{r} 33 \\ \times 29 \\ \hline \end{array}$ | $\begin{array}{r} 90 \\ \times 70 \\ \hline \end{array}$ |
| **3.** | $\begin{array}{r} 57 \\ \times 23 \\ \hline \end{array}$ | $\begin{array}{r} 18 \\ \times 18 \\ \hline \end{array}$ | $\begin{array}{r} 77 \\ \times 27 \\ \hline \end{array}$ | $\begin{array}{r} 65 \\ \times 17 \\ \hline \end{array}$ | $\begin{array}{r} 88 \\ \times 22 \\ \hline \end{array}$ | $\begin{array}{r} 90 \\ \times 20 \\ \hline \end{array}$ |
| **4.** | $\begin{array}{r} 37 \\ \times 23 \\ \hline \end{array}$ | $\begin{array}{r} 91 \\ \times 38 \\ \hline \end{array}$ | $\begin{array}{r} 44 \\ \times 43 \\ \hline \end{array}$ | $\begin{array}{r} 17 \\ \times 13 \\ \hline \end{array}$ | $\begin{array}{r} 88 \\ \times 17 \\ \hline \end{array}$ | $\begin{array}{r} 55 \\ \times 38 \\ \hline \end{array}$ |

# Multiplication Practice

Multiply.

|  | a | b | c | d | e | f |
|---|---|---|---|---|---|---|
| 1. | 45 ×23 | 53 ×17 | 25 ×47 | 48 ×34 | 54 ×23 | 32 ×51 |
| 2. | 35 ×63 | 44 ×29 | 58 ×37 | 39 ×14 | 62 ×46 | 36 ×52 |
| 3. | 57 ×32 | 49 ×27 | 24 ×68 | 37 ×43 | 71 ×54 | 35 ×42 |
| 4. | 56 ×23 | 39 ×32 | 23 ×64 | 43 ×35 | 37 ×19 | 42 ×37 |

# Multiplication Practice

Multiply.

|  | a | b | c | d | e | f |
|---|---|---|---|---|---|---|
| **1.** | 45<br>×38 | 28<br>×57 | 47<br>×63 | 36<br>×82 | 53<br>×74 | 63<br>×28 |
| **2.** | 39<br>×45 | 84<br>×53 | 28<br>×39 | 65<br>×83 | 48<br>×63 | 67<br>×25 |
| **3.** | 27<br>×49 | 82<br>×36 | 24<br>×93 | 48<br>×30 | 83<br>×62 | 46<br>×81 |
| **4.** | 57<br>×38 | 62<br>×54 | 76<br>×46 | 49<br>×73 | 54<br>×18 | 74<br>×36 |

# Multiplication Practice

Multiply.

|     | a | b | c | d |
|-----|------|------|------|------|
| 1.  | 45<br>×27 | 62<br>×39 | 28<br>×45 | 76<br>×66 |
| 2.  | 25<br>×13 | 59<br>×32 | 80<br>×93 | 14<br>×37 |
| 3.  | 97<br>×48 | 92<br>×82 | 58<br>×32 | 91<br>×54 |
| 4.  | 12<br>×61 | 94<br>×27 | 75<br>×69 | 50<br>×37 |
| 5.  | 76<br>×83 | 92<br>×62 | 15<br>×41 | 39<br>×74 |

# Multiplication Practice

Multiply.

|  | a | b | c | d | e |
|---|---|---|---|---|---|
| **1.** | 78<br>×39 | 56<br>×28 | 97<br>×59 | 48<br>×78 | 25<br>×49 |
| **2.** | 98<br>×98 | 78<br>×15 | 48<br>×36 | 77<br>×54 | 83<br>×27 |
| **3.** | 70<br>×36 | 89<br>×18 | 15<br>×48 | 47<br>×32 | 50<br>×78 |
| **4.** | 35<br>×42 | 20<br>×42 | 72<br>×68 | 59<br>×24 | 24<br>×50 |

# Multiplication Practice

Multiply.

| | a | b | c | d | e |
|---|---|---|---|---|---|
| **1.** | 315<br>× 30 | 527<br>× 42 | 287<br>× 21 | 242<br>× 70 | 209<br>× 30 |
| **2.** | 140<br>× 32 | 196<br>× 23 | 673<br>× 92 | 542<br>× 48 | 604<br>× 40 |
| **3.** | 713<br>× 67 | 900<br>× 42 | 198<br>× 72 | 513<br>× 58 | 841<br>× 71 |
| **4.** | 125<br>× 73 | 706<br>× 31 | 448<br>× 33 | 809<br>× 12 | 615<br>× 73 |

# Multiplication Practice

Multiply.

|  | a | b | c | d | e |
|---|---|---|---|---|---|
| 1. | 326<br>× 14 | 345<br>× 23 | 265<br>× 13 | 416<br>× 25 | 364<br>× 18 |
| 2. | 516<br>× 32 | 365<br>× 41 | 423<br>× 51 | 363<br>× 23 | 245<br>× 34 |
| 3. | 523<br>× 15 | 142<br>× 28 | 212<br>× 45 | 234<br>× 36 | 325<br>× 24 |
| 4. | 232<br>× 19 | 425<br>× 43 | 443<br>× 24 | 312<br>× 52 | 286<br>× 34 |

# Multiplication Practice

Multiply.

|  | a | b | c | d | e |
|---|---|---|---|---|---|
| 1. | 407<br>× 39 | 530<br>× 62 | 261<br>× 40 | 704<br>× 82 | 607<br>× 53 |
| 2. | 437<br>× 20 | 623<br>× 30 | 140<br>× 57 | 210<br>× 78 | 527<br>× 30 |
| 3. | 708<br>× 23 | 283<br>× 40 | 340<br>× 68 | 630<br>× 24 | 208<br>× 40 |
| 4. | 896<br>× 30 | 730<br>× 52 | 347<br>× 80 | 310<br>× 64 | 488<br>× 20 |

# Multiplication Practice

Multiply.

|  | a | b | c | d | e |
|---|---|---|---|---|---|
| 1. | 436<br>× 28 | 327<br>× 51 | 824<br>× 32 | 528<br>× 63 | 232<br>× 82 |
| 2. | 329<br>× 18 | 252<br>× 45 | 362<br>× 54 | 243<br>× 84 | 392<br>× 41 |
| 3. | 354<br>× 25 | 236<br>× 57 | 583<br>× 32 | 442<br>× 23 | 623<br>× 52 |
| 4. | 542<br>× 78 | 525<br>× 43 | 514<br>× 62 | 362<br>× 54 | 424<br>× 49 |

# Multiplication Practice

Multiply.

|   | a | b | c | d | e |
|---|---|---|---|---|---|
| 1. | 43 ×42 | 75 ×12 | 52 ×28 | 36 ×91 | 16 ×77 |
| 2. | 24 ×87 | 62 ×54 | 96 ×32 | 18 ×47 | 33 ×79 |
| 3. | 26 ×53 | 39 ×74 | 44 ×81 | 473 × 64 | 856 × 22 |
| 4. | 838 × 58 | 266 × 93 | 372 × 46 | 659 × 78 | 428 × 37 |

**SCORE** ◯ **/ 20**

# Multiplication Practice

Multiply.

|  | a | b | c | d | e |
|---|---|---|---|---|---|
| **1.** | 28<br>×24 | 35<br>×18 | 26<br>×33 | 85<br>×45 | 43<br>×62 |
| **2.** | 482<br>× 26 | 49<br>×54 | 263<br>× 84 | 132<br>× 68 | 164<br>× 42 |
| **3.** | 324<br>× 27 | 816<br>× 16 | 255<br>× 44 | 165<br>× 23 | 66<br>×71 |
| **4.** | 150<br>× 22 | 182<br>× 12 | 324<br>× 36 | 522<br>× 63 | 38<br>×24 |

# Multiplication Practice

Multiply.

|  | a | b | c | d | e |
|---|---|---|---|---|---|
| 1. | 627<br>× 28 | 205<br>× 67 | 364<br>× 42 | 423<br>× 57 | 920<br>× 84 |
| 2. | 549<br>× 30 | 847<br>× 27 | 925<br>× 56 | 427<br>× 93 | 240<br>× 64 |
| 3. | 149<br>× 80 | 847<br>× 92 | 148<br>× 24 | 492<br>× 76 | 284<br>× 33 |
| 4. | 620<br>× 34 | 413<br>× 47 | 404<br>× 76 | 243<br>× 91 | 128<br>× 24 |
| 5. | 136<br>× 58 | 132<br>× 49 | 149<br>× 26 | 427<br>× 78 | 264<br>× 32 |

# Multiplication Practice

Multiply.

|  | a | b | c | d | e |
|---|---|---|---|---|---|
| 1. | 24<br>×75 | 936<br>× 47 | 365<br>× 28 | 573<br>× 65 | 92<br>×84 |
| 2. | 476<br>× 83 | 468<br>× 57 | 23<br>×92 | 645<br>× 73 | 765<br>× 48 |
| 3. | 59<br>×63 | 368<br>× 87 | 28<br>×61 | 537<br>× 44 | 804<br>× 87 |
| 4. | 48<br>×29 | 37<br>×73 | 725<br>× 52 | 39<br>×38 | 457<br>× 86 |

# Multiplication Practice

Multiply.

|  | a | b | c | d | e |
|---|---|---|---|---|---|
| **1.** | 467 × 35 | 538 × 47 | 393 × 82 | 724 × 56 | 821 × 75 |
| **2.** | 463 × 43 | 522 × 68 | 326 × 92 | 735 × 45 | 268 × 39 |
| **3.** | 534 × 76 | 232 × 98 | 845 × 63 | 928 × 81 | 625 × 33 |
| **4.** | 856 × 42 | 932 × 58 | 734 × 54 | 487 × 72 | 289 × 79 |

# Estimating Products

Round each number to its highest place value.

$$3764 \longrightarrow 4000$$
$$\times 247 \longrightarrow \times 200$$
$$\overline{800000}$$

$4 \times 2 = 8$
$4 \times 20 = 80$
$4 \times 200 = 800$

$40 \times 2 = 8$
$400 \times 20 = 8000$
$4000 \times 200 = 800000$

---

Estimate the product.

|  | a | b | c | d | e |
|---|---|---|---|---|---|
| **1.** | 76 ×2 | 38 ×5 | 21 ×9 | 461 ×3 | 728 ×4 |
| **2.** | 15 ×3 | 83 ×8 | 14 ×6 | 5789 ×7 | 8365 ×9 |
| **3.** | 56 ×32 | 89 ×25 | 41 ×27 | 95 ×63 | 75 ×18 |
| **4.** | 294 ×51 | 729 ×44 | 129 ×37 | 381 ×23 | 897 ×68 |

# Check What You Learned

## Multiplying through 3 Digits by 2 Digits

Multiply.

|   | a | b | c | d | e | f | g |
|---|---|---|---|---|---|---|---|
| 1. | 72 $\times 14$ | 24 $\times 68$ | 339 $\times\ 42$ | 34 $\times 28$ | 150 $\times\ 19$ | 333 $\times\ \ 22$ | 93 $\times 42$ |
| 2. | 42 $\times 62$ | 64 $\times 18$ | 31 $\times 27$ | 300 $\times\ 21$ | 72 $\times 94$ | 73 $\times 28$ | 90 $\times 28$ |
| 3. | 81 $\times 76$ | 728 $\times\ 61$ | 22 $\times 43$ | 207 $\times\ 21$ | 90 $\times 56$ | 79 $\times 44$ | 643 $\times\ 37$ |
| 4. | 743 $\times\ 12$ | 439 $\times\ 10$ | 117 $\times\ 23$ | 43 $\times 46$ | 84 $\times 65$ | 20 $\times 19$ | 555 $\times\ 40$ |
| 5. | 42 $\times 41$ | 311 $\times\ 12$ | 72 $\times 18$ | 12 $\times 11$ | 50 $\times 42$ | 95 $\times 27$ | 353 $\times\ 17$ |
| 6. | 606 $\times\ 12$ | 786 $\times\ 31$ | 202 $\times\ 33$ | 52 $\times 49$ | 86 $\times 14$ | 94 $\times 65$ | 403 $\times\ 55$ |

## Check What You Know

## Problem Solving: Multiplying through 3 Digits by 2 Digits

Read the problem carefully and solve. Show your work under each question.

Students in Thorton's schools are collecting soda cans and bottles for a charity drive. They have a contest to see which students and which schools collect the most cans and bottles.

1. Elmhurst has 328 students. Each student collects 28 cans during the contest. How many cans do the students collect altogether?


   _____ cans


2. At Oakwood, 47 students collect 125 bottles each. How many bottles do the students collect in all?


   _____ bottles


3. Park Central has 156 students. Each student collects 14 bottles. How many bottles do they collect in total?


   _____ bottles


4. The contest lasts 15 weeks. One student, Raul, collects 33 cans per week. How many cans does Raul collect during the contest?


   _____ cans

# Multiplying 2 Digits by 2 Digits

Read the problem carefully and solve. Show your work under each question.

Olivia's Orchards grows two types of apples. One type is red and the other is green. The trees that grow red apples are planted in 34 rows with 68 trees in each row. The trees that grow green apples are planted in 26 rows with 47 trees in each row.

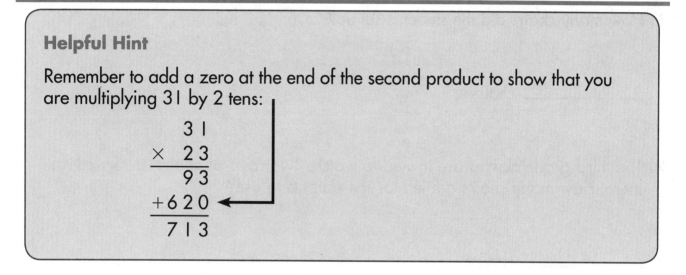

**Helpful Hint**

Remember to add a zero at the end of the second product to show that you are multiplying 31 by 2 tens:

$$
\begin{array}{r}
31 \\
\times\ 23 \\
\hline
93 \\
+620 \\
\hline
713
\end{array}
$$

**1.** How many of the trees in the orchard grow red apples?

_____ trees

**2.** What is the total number of trees in the orchard that grow green apples?

_____ trees

**3.** The orchard decides to rope off three rows of red apple trees for a school group to go apple picking. How many red apple trees are not roped off?

_____ red apple trees

# Multiplying 2 Digits by 2 Digits

Read the problem carefully and solve. Show your work under each question.

Ramon's fourth grade class performs a play for their parents. Ramon and other students help set up chairs for the performance. They set up 13 rows of chairs and each row has 21 chairs.

**1.** How many chairs did the students set up?

_____ chairs

**2.** The third grade classes are invited to watch. Two rows of chairs are saved for them. How many chairs are left for the parents to use?

_____ chairs

**3.** Before the play starts, the principal decides to add 2 more chairs to each row. How many total chairs are there now?

_____ chairs

**SCORE ⬭ /8**

# Multiplying 2 Digits by 2 Digits

Solve each problem. Show your work under each question.

**1.** There are 24 hours in one day. How many hours are there in 18 days?

There are _____ hours in a day.

There are _____ hours in 18 days.

**2.** It takes 47 apples to fill a bushel. There are 24 bushels to fill. How many apples does the farmer need to fill all the bushels?

There are _____ apples in a bushel.

There are _____ bushels to fill.

The farmer needs _____ apples to fill all the bushels.

**3.** Bob's car can go 23 miles on one gallon of gas. The gas tank holds 26 gallons. How many miles can Bob's car go on a full tank of gas?

Bob's car can go _____ miles on one gallon.

The car holds _____ gallons of gas.

It can go _____ miles on a full tank of gas.

# Multiplying 2 Digits by 2 Digits

Solve each problem. Show your work under each question.

**1.** Buses were reserved for a field trip. If each bus holds 20 students, how many students would 16 buses hold?

The buses would hold _____ students.

**2.** If 16 potato chips is a serving size and there are 15 servings in a bag, how many potato chips are in each bag?

There are _____ chips in a bag.

**3.** There are 48 cabins at summer camp. If each cabin holds 25 campers, how many campers are at summer camp?

There are _____ campers at summer camp.

# Multiplying 2 Digits by 2 Digits

Solve each problem. Show your work under each question.

1. On Monday, the amusement park offered tickets for 10 dollars. In the first hour, 96 people bought tickets for the park. How much money did the park make on ticket sales in the first hour?

The amusement park made _____ dollars in the first hour.

2. Mr. Tao taught mathematics to classes of 37 students for 27 years. How many students has Mr. Tao taught in all?

Mr. Tao has taught _____ students.

3. If Latisha brushes her teeth 14 times a week, how many times will Latisha have brushed her teeth in 72 weeks?

Latisha will have brushed her teeth _____ times.

# Multiplying 3 Digits by 2 Digits

Read the problem carefully and solve. Show your work under each question.

Meiko researches the buildings in her city. The tallest building has 43 floors and 219 windows on each floor. Meiko's father, Mr. Arimoto, works in the building across the street. His building has 27 floors and 128 windows on each floor.

**1.** How many total windows does the tallest building have?

_____ windows

**2.** How many total windows does the building Mr. Arimoto works in have?

_____ windows

**3.** Window washers washed the windows on 8 floors of Mr. Arimoto's building. How many windows do they have left to wash?

_____ windows

# Multiplying 3 Digits by 2 Digits

Solve each problem. Show your work under each question.

1. Florence recently opened 29 candle shops. In each shop, she stocked 165 candles. How many candles has Florence stocked in all the shops?

Florence has stocked _____ candles in all.

2. There are 24 movie frames for one second of film. There are 723 seconds in a cartoon. How many frames are there total for the whole cartoon?

There are _____ frames.

3. Harmony Corporation planted 114 trees in 42 cities across the United States. How many total trees did Harmony Corporation plant?

Harmony Corporation planted _____ trees.

# Multiplication Practice

Solve each problem. Show your work under each question.

**1.** The hardward store contains 56 shelves of paint. There are 32 cans of paint on each shelf. How many total cans of paint are there?

There are _____ total cans of paint.

**2.** If the library loans 726 books a day, how many books will the library have loaned after 21 days?

The library will have loaned _____ books.

**3.** The factory produces 274 sweaters in a day. How many sweaters will it produce in 59 days?

The factory will produce _____ sweaters.

## Multiplication Practice

Solve each problem. Show your work under each question.

1. A freight train carries 153 boxes of soap. Each box weighs 44 pounds. How many pounds of soap is the train carrying?

   The train is carrying _____ pounds of soap.

2. The Haws Corporation has 45 employees. Each employee works 705 hours a year. What are the total number of employee hours a year for the Haws Corporation?

   There are _____ employee hours a year.

3. Each spring, Zara helps her mom plant flowers. There are 24 rows of flowers and she plants 18 flowers in each row. How many flowers does Zara plant?

   Zara plants _____ flowers.

# Estimating Products

Read the problem carefully and solve. Show your work under each question.

A hardware store sells many kinds of products. The owners of the store often estimate how fast the products are selling, so they know when to buy more of each product they sell.

---

**Helpful Hint**

To estimate the product of two numbers, round each number to its highest place value.

Suppose you want to estimate the product of 837 times 36. Round 837 to 800. Round 36 to 40. Then, multiply 800 times 40. The product is 32,000.

---

1. The store sells an average of 17 boxes of nails per day. The store is open 311 days per year. About how many boxes of nails are sold in a year?


   about _____ boxes


2. Simon sells about 2 tape measures per week. There are 104 weeks in 2 years. About how many tape measures does Simon sell in 2 years?


   about _____ tape measures

# Estimating Products

**3.** Jason sells an average of 56 faucets per month. About how many faucets does he sell in 48 months?

about _____ faucets

**4.** Pearl sells an average of 14 brooms per month. What is an estimate for the number of brooms she sells in a year?

about _____ brooms

# Check What You Learned

## Problem Solving: Multiplying through 3 Digits by 2 Digits

Read the problem carefully and solve. Show your work under each question.

The city of Alford has 315 firefighters. During each shift, firefighters are at the station for 3 days in a row. Then, they have 4 days off. They also get 4 weeks of vacation per year.

1. All the firefighters get paid for vacation each year. How many total weeks of vacation does the city pay the firefighters each year?

    _____ weeks

2. Julia knows that a firefighter works 72 hours every week and 48 weeks per year. About how many total hours does each firefighter work per year?

    about _____ hours

3. There are 72 hours in 3 days. How many total hours do 125 firefighters work in 3 days?

    _____ hours

4. Each firefighter in Alford misses 3 days of work per year because of sickness. How many days in total do all of the firefighters miss per year?

    _____ days

# Final Test Chapters 1–4

Multiply.

|  | a | b | c | d | e |
|---|---|---|---|---|---|
| 1. | 7<br>×8 | 9<br>×4 | 7<br>×4 | 8<br>×6 | 21<br>× 4 |
| 2. | 232<br>× 3 | 14<br>× 2 | 44<br>× 2 | 120<br>× 4 | 20<br>× 4 |
| 3. | 32<br>× 7 | 47<br>× 3 | 1321<br>× 8 | 40<br>× 9 | 7217<br>× 9 |
| 4. | 9648<br>× 7 | 72<br>× 8 | 384<br>× 4 | 25<br>× 7 | 49<br>× 9 |
| 5. | 11<br>×10 | 22<br>×11 | 31<br>×32 | 43<br>×20 | 50<br>×10 |
| 6. | 75<br>×25 | 32<br>×18 | 132<br>× 41 | 81<br>×37 | 103<br>× 17 |
| 7. | 418<br>× 45 | 500<br>× 32 | 199<br>× 47 | 578<br>× 23 | 887<br>× 52 |

# Final Test  Chapters 1–4

Multiply.

|  | a | b | c | d | e | f |
|---|---|---|---|---|---|---|
| 8. | 9<br>×6 | 34<br>×29 | 14<br>× 2 | 987<br>× 4 | 66<br>×34 | 83<br>×12 |
| 9. | 645<br>× 24 | 1239<br>× 5 | 8<br>×8 | 459<br>× 56 | 99<br>×30 | 4372<br>× 7 |
| 10. | 11<br>× 3 | 400<br>× 25 | 78<br>×62 | 65<br>×97 | 325<br>× 88 | 348<br>× 9 |
| 11. | 10<br>×10 | 6<br>×4 | 584<br>× 43 | 8934<br>× 5 | 34<br>×65 | 23<br>× 5 |
| 12. | 16<br>× 8 | 2346<br>× 2 | 432<br>× 87 | 3491<br>× 3 | 27<br>×48 | 1256<br>× 70 |

Estimate the product.

|  | a | b | c | d | e | f |
|---|---|---|---|---|---|---|
| 13. | 46<br>× 3 | 98<br>× 7 | 234<br>× 9 | 23<br>×14 | 18<br>× 2 | 173<br>× 23 |
| 14. | 432<br>× 53 | 7832<br>× 24 | 498<br>× 23 | 87<br>×49 | 237<br>× 56 | 132<br>× 78 |

# Final Test Chapters 1–4

Multiply.

|  | a | b | c | d | e | f |
|---|---|---|---|---|---|---|
| **15.** | 81<br>× 9 | 23<br>× 4 | 63<br>× 7 | 22<br>× 3 | 78<br>× 9 | 94<br>× 3 |
| **16.** | 90<br>× 8 | 36<br>× 5 | 52<br>× 3 | 44<br>× 2 | 73<br>× 5 | 87<br>× 8 |
| **17.** | 465<br>× 3 | 203<br>× 3 | 515<br>× 8 | 150<br>× 3 | 8917<br>× 7 | 711<br>× 6 |
| **18.** | 258<br>× 4 | 6412<br>× 3 | 330<br>× 3 | 703<br>× 6 | 2900<br>× 9 | 664<br>× 8 |

Find the rule and complete the table.

a

**19.**

| In | Out |
|----|-----|
| 1 | |
| 2 | |
| 3 | 26 |
| 4 | 34 |
| 5 | |

_____

b

| In | Out |
|----|-----|
| 3 | |
| 5 | 23 |
| 7 | |
| 9 | |
| 11 | 53 |

_____

c

| In | Out |
|----|-----|
| 1 | |
| 4 | 43 |
| 7 | |
| 8 | |
| 10 | 103 |

_____

**Final Test** Chapters 1–4

Solve each problem. Show your work under each question.

**20.** Xavier loves to eat pears. He ate 2 a day for 48 days. How many pears did Xavier eat?

Xavier ate _____ pears.

**21.** Clayton keeps pet mice. If his 33 mice have 12 babies each, how many mice will Clayton have in all?

Clayton will have _____ mice.

**22.** In a tropical rain forest, the average annual rainfall is about 150 inches. After 5 years, about how much rain will have fallen in the rain forest?

About _____ inches of rain will have fallen.

**23.** A class of 55 students went on a field trip to collect seashells. If the students collected 15 shells each, how many shells did they collect?

The students collected _____ shells.

**24.** What is the next number in this pattern? Explain your answer.

3, 12, 57, 282, 1407 _____

# Final Test Chapters 1–4

Solve each problem. Show your work under each question.

**25.** Mrs. Rockwell checked on how much time her students spend doing homework. If all 23 students spend 20 hours each week, how much homework do the students do in a week?

They do _____ hours of homework a week.

**26.** A cable program loans channel boxes to 21 community centers for a trial program. If there are 12 boxes for each center, how many boxes are being loaned?

There are _____ boxes being loaned.

**27.** A girls' club is trying to get into the record books for the most hair braids. There are 372 girls. If each girl braids her hair into 40 little braids, how many braids will they have?

They will have _____ braids.

**28.** In one week, Pop sold ice cream cones to 2,375 people. If each customer had 2 scoops, how many scoops did Pop sell?

Pop sold _____ scoops of ice cream.

## Final Test Chapters 1–4

Solve each problem. Show your work under each question.

29. Students set up the chairs for the spring concert at Bethel High School. There were 25 rows with 10 chairs in each row. How many chairs did they set up?

   They set up _____ chairs.

30. The Ferris wheel at the fair gave 198 rides on opening day. If each ticket was good for 2 rides, how many tickets were used to ride the Ferris wheel? Write a multiplication equation to find how many tickets were used. Then, solve.

   _____

   _____ tickets were used to ride the Ferris wheel.

31. At the Bead Shop, there are 25 rows of glass beads. If there are 320 glass beads in each row, how many glass beads are in the shop?

   There are _____ glass beads in the shop.

32. The cafeteria planned to bake 3 chocolate chip cookies for every student in the school. If there are 2,715 students, how many cookies does the cafeteria need to bake?

   The cafeteria needs to bake _____ cookies.

# Scoring Record for Pretests, Posttests, Mid-Test, and Final Test

| Pretests, Posttests, Mid-Test, and Final Test | Your Score | Performance | | | |
|---|---|---|---|---|---|
| | | Excellent | Very Good | Fair | Needs Improvement |
| Chapter 1 Pretest | ____ of 30 | 28–30 | 24–27 | 18–23 | 17 or fewer |
| Chapter 1 Posttest | ____ of 30 | 28–30 | 24–27 | 18–23 | 17 or fewer |
| Chapter 2 Pretest | ____ of 4 | 4 | 3 | 2 | 1 |
| Chapter 2 Posttest | ____ of 5 | 5 | 4 | 3 | 2 or fewer |
| Chapter 3 Pretest | ____ of 48 | 46–48 | 39–45 | 30–38 | 29 or fewer |
| Chapter 3 Posttest | ____ of 42 | 40–42 | 35–39 | 26–34 | 25 or fewer |
| Chapter 4 Pretest | ____ of 4 | 4 | 3 | 2 | 1 |
| Chapter 4 Posttest | ____ of 4 | 4 | 3 | 2 | 1 |
| Mid-Test | ____ of 39 | 37–39 | 32–36 | 24–31 | 23 or fewer |
| Final Test | ____ of 125 | 119–125 | 100–118 | 75–99 | 74 or fewer |

Record your test score in the Your Score column. See where your score falls in the Performance columns. Your score is based on the total number of required responses. If your score is fair or needs improvement, review the chapter material.

# Answer Key

---

## Page 5 — Check What You Know: Multiplying through 4 Digits by 1 Digit

| | a | b | c | d | e |
|---|---|---|---|---|---|
| 1. | 37 × 4 = 148 | 8 × 3 = 24 | 75 × 2 = 150 | 6 × 5 = 30 | 68 × 2 = 136 |
| 2. | 76 × 2 = 152 | 359 × 4 = 1436 | 34 × 6 = 204 | 638 × 5 = 3190 | 48 × 2 = 96 |
| 3. | 45 × 6 = 270 | 2467 × 3 = 7401 | 43 × 4 = 172 | 5 × 2 = 10 | 839 × 5 = 4195 |
| 4. | 64 × 3 = 192 | 83 × 6 = 498 | 45 × 3 = 135 | 4363 × 5 = 21815 | 93 × 4 = 372 |
| 5. | 6 × 2 = 12 | 473 × 5 = 2365 | 5966 × 4 = 23864 | 25 × 6 = 150 | 4874 × 3 = 14622 |
| 6. | 923 × 6 = 5538 | 97 × 2 = 194 | 447 × 5 = 2235 | 77 × 4 = 308 | 84 × 4 = 336 |

**5**

---

## Page 6 — Understanding Multiplication

two times seven: 2 × 7 means 7 + 7 → 7 factor, × 2 factor, 14 product (7 + 7 = 14)

five times three: 5 × 3 means 5 + 5 + 5 → 5 factor, × 3 factor, 15 product (5 + 5 + 5 = 15)

Multiply. Write the corresponding addition problem next to each multiplication problem.

| | a | b | c | d | e |
|---|---|---|---|---|---|
| 1. | 3 × 2 = 6 (3+3) | 7 × 2 = 14 (7+7) | 6 × 2 = 12 (6+6) | 9 × 2 = 18 (9+9) | 8 × 2 = 16 (8+8) |
| 2. | 2 × 2 = 4 (2+2) | 1 × 2 = 2 (1+1) | 5 × 3 = 15 (5+5+5) | 6 × 3 = 18 (6+6+6) | 3 × 3 = 9 (3+3+3) |
| 3. | 2 × 3 = 6 (2+2+2) | 1 × 3 = 3 (1+1+1) | 4 × 3 = 12 (4+4+4) | 7 × 3 = 21 (7+7+7) | 2 × 4 = 8 (2+2+2+2) |
| 4. | 4 × 4 = 16 (4+4+4+4) | 1 × 4 = 4 (1+1+1+1) | 5 × 4 = 20 (5+5+5+5) | 9 × 4 = 36 (9+9+9+9) | 8 × 4 = 32 (8+8+8+8) |

**6**

---

## Page 7 — Multiplying Single Digits

factor 7 → Find the 7-column. factor 3 → Find the 3-row. product 21 → The product is named where the 7-column and the 3-row meet.

Use the table to multiply.

| | a | b | c | d | e | f |
|---|---|---|---|---|---|---|
| 1. | 3 × 3 = 9 | 8 × 7 = 56 | 2 × 9 = 18 | 7 × 5 = 35 | 9 × 4 = 36 | 6 × 6 = 36 |
| 2. | 9 × 9 = 81 | 4 × 3 = 12 | 5 × 3 = 15 | 4 × 4 = 16 | 7 × 7 = 49 | 9 × 3 = 27 |
| 3. | 5 × 8 = 40 | 6 × 4 = 24 | 8 × 2 = 16 | 9 × 7 = 63 | 4 × 8 = 32 | 7 × 3 = 21 |
| 4. | 9 × 1 = 9 | 9 × 5 = 45 | 8 × 6 = 48 | 7 × 6 = 42 | 9 × 6 = 54 | 7 × 8 = 56 |

**7**

---

## Page 8 — Multiplying Single Digits

Fill in the missing number.

| | a | b | c | d | e |
|---|---|---|---|---|---|
| 1. | 6 × 9 = 54 | 7 × 6 = 42 | 5 × 5 = 25 | 1 × 5 = 5 | 8 × 9 = 72 |
| 2. | 4 × 4 = 16 | 2 × 4 = 8 | 3 × 6 = 18 | 7 × 7 = 49 | 3 × 2 = 6 |
| 3. | 8 × 7 = 56 | 8 × 3 = 24 | 8 × 3 = 24 | 9 × 7 = 63 | 5 × 6 = 30 |
| 4. | 3 × 5 = 15 | 8 × 8 = 64 | 4 × 8 = 32 | 9 × 5 = 45 | 1 × 8 = 8 |

**8**

---

## Page 9 — Multiplying 2 Digits by 1 Digit

32 × 3 : Multiply 2 ones by 3. 2 × 3 = 6 → 6
32 × 3 : Multiply 3 tens by 3. 30 × 3 = 90 → 96

Multiply.

| | a | b | c | d | e | f |
|---|---|---|---|---|---|---|
| 1. | 23 × 2 = 46 | 71 × 1 = 71 | 12 × 4 = 48 | 33 × 2 = 66 | 10 × 7 = 70 | 24 × 2 = 48 |
| 2. | 44 × 2 = 88 | 43 × 2 = 86 | 90 × 1 = 90 | 22 × 4 = 88 | 12 × 3 = 36 | 14 × 2 = 28 |
| 3. | 11 × 9 = 99 | 75 × 1 = 75 | 11 × 6 = 66 | 30 × 3 = 90 | 10 × 4 = 40 | 42 × 2 = 84 |
| 4. | 11 × 7 = 77 | 10 × 2 = 20 | 33 × 0 = 0 | 13 × 3 = 39 | 20 × 3 = 60 | 31 × 2 = 62 |

**9**

---

## Page 10 — Multiplication Practice

Multiply.

| | a | b | c | d | e | f |
|---|---|---|---|---|---|---|
| 1. | 10 × 2 = 20 | 41 × 2 = 82 | 13 × 2 = 26 | 40 × 2 = 80 | 30 × 2 = 60 | 11 × 5 = 55 |
| 2. | 30 × 1 = 30 | 11 × 7 = 77 | 25 × 1 = 25 | 42 × 0 = 0 | 22 × 3 = 66 | 10 × 1 = 10 |
| 3. | 14 × 0 = 0 | 10 × 5 = 50 | 31 × 3 = 93 | 12 × 3 = 36 | 20 × 4 = 80 | 10 × 7 = 70 |

Find the rule and complete each table.

4.

a — multiply by 5 and add 1

| In | Out |
|---|---|
| 2 | 11 |
| 3 | 16 |
| 4 | 21 |
| 5 | 26 |
| 6 | 31 |

b — multiply by 9 and subtract 2

| In | Out |
|---|---|
| 1 | 7 |
| 3 | 25 |
| 5 | 43 |
| 7 | 61 |
| 9 | 79 |

c — multiply by 6 and add 6

| In | Out |
|---|---|
| 2 | 18 |
| 4 | 30 |
| 5 | 36 |
| 7 | 48 |
| 9 | 60 |

**10**

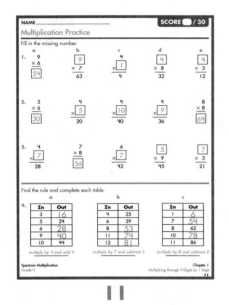

**Page 11 — Multiplication Practice** (SCORE / 30)

Fill in the missing number.

1. a) 9 × 6 = **54**  b) **9** × 7 = 63  c) 4 × **1** = 4  d) 4 × 8 = 32  e) 4 × 3 = 12
2. a) 5 × 6 = **30**  b) 4 × **5** = 20  c) 4 × **10** = 40  d) 4 × **9** = 36  e) 8 × 8 = **64**
3. a) 4 × **7** = 28  b) 7 × 8 = **56**  c) 6 × **7** = 42  d) **5** × 9 = 45  e) **7** × 3 = 21

Find the rule and complete each table.

| a In | Out |
|---|---|
| 3 | 16 |
| 5 | 24 |
| 6 | 28 |
| 9 | 40 |
| 10 | 44 |

multiply by 4 and add 4

| b In | Out |
|---|---|
| 4 | 25 |
| 6 | 39 |
| 8 | 53 |
| 11 | 74 |
| 12 | 81 |

multiply by 7 and subtract 3

| c In | Out |
|---|---|
| 1 | 6 |
| 7 | 54 |
| 8 | 62 |
| 10 | 78 |
| 11 | 86 |

multiply by 8 and subtract 2

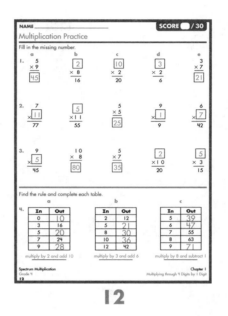

**Page 12 — Multiplication Practice** (SCORE / 30)

Fill in the missing number.

1. a) 5 × 9 = **45**  b) **2** × 8 = 16  c) **10** × 2 = 20  d) 3 × 2 = 6  e) 3 × 7 = **21**
2. a) 7 × **11** = 77  b) **5** × 11 = 55  c) 5 × 5 = **25**  d) 9 × **1** = 9  e) 6 × **7** = 42
3. a) 9 × **5** = 45  b) 10 × 8 = **80**  c) 5 × 7 = **35**  d) 2 × **10** = 20  e) **5** × 3 = 15

Find the rule and complete each table.

| a In | Out |
|---|---|
| 0 | 10 |
| 3 | 16 |
| 5 | 20 |
| 7 | 24 |
| 9 | 28 |

multiply by 2 and add 10

| b In | Out |
|---|---|
| 2 | 12 |
| 5 | 21 |
| 8 | 30 |
| 10 | 36 |
| 12 | 42 |

multiply by 3 and add 6

| c In | Out |
|---|---|
| 5 | 39 |
| 6 | 47 |
| 7 | 55 |
| 8 | 63 |
| 9 | 71 |

multiply by 8 and subtract 1

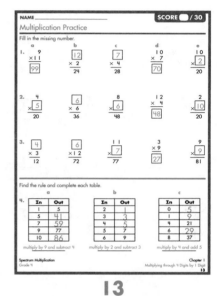

**Page 13 — Multiplication Practice** (SCORE / 30)

Fill in the missing number.

1. a) **11** × 9 = 99  b) **12** × 2 = 24  c) **7** × 4 = 28  d) 10 × 7 = **70**  e) 10 × **2** = 20
2. a) **4** × 5 = 20  b) **6** × 6 = 36  c) 8 × **6** = 48  d) 12 × 4 = **48**  e) 2 × **10** = 20
3. a) **4** × 3 = 12  b) **6** × 12 = 72  c) 11 × **7** = 77  d) 3 × 9 = **27**  e) 9 × **9** = 81

Find the rule and complete each table.

| a In | Out |
|---|---|
| 1 | 5 |
| 5 | 41 |
| 7 | 59 |
| 9 | 77 |
| 10 | 86 |

multiply by 9 and subtract 4

| b In | Out |
|---|---|
| 2 | 1 |
| 3 | 3 |
| 4 | 5 |
| 5 | 7 |
| 6 | 9 |

multiply by 2 and subtract 3

| c In | Out |
|---|---|
| 0 | 5 |
| 1 | 9 |
| 4 | 21 |
| 6 | 29 |
| 8 | 37 |

multiply by 4 and add 5

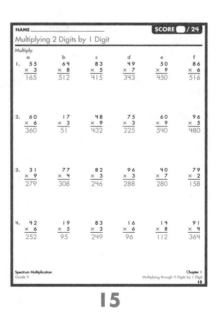

**Page 14 — Multiplying 2 Digits by 1 Digit** (SCORE / 24)

Multiply.
1. a) 73 × 4 = 292  b) 25 × 2 = 50  c) 36 × 3 = 108  d) 52 × 5 = 260  e) 23 × 4 = 92  f) 42 × 5 = 210
2. a) 19 × 2 = 38  b) 26 × 2 = 52  c) 68 × 3 = 204  d) 54 × 5 = 270  e) 47 × 8 = 376  f) 33 × 4 = 132
3. a) 32 × 9 = 288  b) 48 × 8 = 384  c) 52 × 3 = 156  d) 34 × 4 = 136  e) 17 × 5 = 85  f) 22 × 5 = 110
4. a) 66 × 3 = 198  b) 45 × 5 = 225  c) 66 × 5 = 330  d) 19 × 9 = 171  e) 38 × 9 = 342  f) 74 × 3 = 222

**Page 15 — Multiplying 2 Digits by 1 Digit** (SCORE / 24)

Multiply.
1. a) 55 × 3 = 165  b) 64 × 8 = 512  c) 83 × 5 = 415  d) 49 × 7 = 343  e) 50 × 9 = 450  f) 86 × 6 = 516
2. a) 60 × 6 = 360  b) 17 × 3 = 51  c) 48 × 9 = 432  d) 75 × 3 = 225  e) 60 × 9 = 540  f) 96 × 5 = 480
3. a) 31 × 9 = 279  b) 77 × 4 = 308  c) 82 × 3 = 246  d) 96 × 3 = 288  e) 40 × 7 = 280  f) 79 × 2 = 158
4. a) 42 × 6 = 252  b) 19 × 5 = 95  c) 83 × 3 = 249  d) 16 × 6 = 96  e) 14 × 8 = 112  f) 91 × 4 = 364

**Page 16 — Multiplication Practice** (SCORE / 24)

Multiply.
1. a) 13 × 5 = 65  b) 38 × 2 = 76  c) 14 × 8 = 112  d) 15 × 6 = 90  e) 36 × 3 = 108  f) 39 × 2 = 78
2. a) 27 × 4 = 108  b) 28 × 3 = 84  c) 47 × 2 = 94  d) 16 × 9 = 144  e) 15 × 5 = 75  f) 13 × 7 = 91
3. a) 17 × 6 = 102  b) 25 × 4 = 100  c) 24 × 3 = 72  d) 45 × 2 = 90  e) 16 × 8 = 128  f) 14 × 7 = 98
4. a) 29 × 2 = 58  b) 16 × 4 = 64  c) 37 × 3 = 111  d) 16 × 5 = 80  e) 48 × 2 = 96  f) 19 × 4 = 76

# Answer Key

## Page 17

NAME _____

**Multiplication Practice** — SCORE /24

Multiply.

| | a | b | c | d | e | f |
|---|---|---|---|---|---|---|
| 1. | 26 ×3 = 78 | 64 ×5 = 320 | 43 ×8 = 344 | 57 ×6 = 342 | 98 ×2 = 196 | 35 ×4 = 140 |
| 2. | 76 ×3 = 228 | 46 ×7 = 322 | 85 ×3 = 255 | 35 ×8 = 280 | 23 ×9 = 207 | 62 ×5 = 310 |
| 3. | 42 ×6 = 252 | 73 ×4 = 292 | 82 ×5 = 410 | 67 ×3 = 201 | 27 ×8 = 216 | 49 ×7 = 343 |
| 4. | 88 ×2 = 176 | 36 ×9 = 324 | 53 ×6 = 318 | 83 ×4 = 332 | 65 ×5 = 325 | 34 ×8 = 272 |

Spectrum Multiplication Grade 4 — Chapter 1, Multiplying through 4 Digits by 1 Digit — 17

## Page 18

**Multiplication Practice** — SCORE /24

Multiply.

| | a | b | c | d | e | f |
|---|---|---|---|---|---|---|
| 1. | 84 ×5 = 420 | 35 ×7 = 245 | 63 ×8 = 504 | 57 ×4 = 228 | 55 ×9 = 495 | 43 ×6 = 258 |
| 2. | 92 ×8 = 736 | 42 ×9 = 378 | 85 ×6 = 510 | 53 ×4 = 212 | 74 ×8 = 592 | 83 ×5 = 415 |
| 3. | 65 ×7 = 455 | 87 ×3 = 261 | 49 ×6 = 294 | 23 ×9 = 207 | 86 ×4 = 344 | 35 ×8 = 280 |
| 4. | 82 ×5 = 410 | 32 ×9 = 288 | 46 ×6 = 276 | 89 ×2 = 178 | 64 ×7 = 448 | 43 ×9 = 387 |

Spectrum Multiplication Grade 4 — Chapter 1, Multiplying through 4 Digits by 1 Digit — 18

## Page 19

**Multiplication Practice** — SCORE /24

Multiply.

| | a | b | c | d | e | f |
|---|---|---|---|---|---|---|
| 1. | 76 ×4 = 304 | 23 ×6 = 138 | 49 ×8 = 392 | 64 ×5 = 320 | 87 ×9 = 783 | 43 ×7 = 301 |
| 2. | 88 ×3 = 264 | 73 ×6 = 438 | 54 ×8 = 432 | 69 ×5 = 345 | 74 ×9 = 666 | 39 ×7 = 273 |
| 3. | 83 ×9 = 747 | 45 ×6 = 270 | 75 ×8 = 600 | 62 ×7 = 434 | 28 ×9 = 252 | 52 ×8 = 416 |
| 4. | 63 ×5 = 315 | 77 ×3 = 231 | 38 ×9 = 342 | 97 ×2 = 194 | 48 ×7 = 336 | 53 ×9 = 477 |

Spectrum Multiplication Grade 4 — Chapter 1, Multiplying through 4 Digits by 1 Digit — 19

## Page 20

**Multiplying 3 Digits by 1 Digit** — SCORE /20

752 ×8 = 6   Multiply 2 ones by 8. Put 1 ten above the 5.
752 ×8 = 16   Multiply 5 tens by 8. Then, add 1 ten. Put 4 hundreds above the 7.
752 ×8 = 6016   Multiply 7 hundreds by 8. Then, add 4 hundreds.

Multiply.

| | a | b | c | d | e |
|---|---|---|---|---|---|
| 1. | 118 ×3 = 354 | 305 ×4 = 1220 | 224 ×5 = 1120 | 152 ×3 = 456 | 200 ×7 = 1400 |
| 2. | 327 ×3 = 981 | 158 ×3 = 474 | 235 ×6 = 1410 | 142 ×9 = 1278 | 580 ×3 = 1740 |
| 3. | 335 ×5 = 1675 | 190 ×7 = 1330 | 421 ×8 = 3368 | 201 ×9 = 1809 | 287 ×3 = 861 |
| 4. | 405 ×5 = 2025 | 118 ×8 = 944 | 402 ×3 = 1206 | 498 ×6 = 2988 | 700 ×7 = 4900 |

Spectrum Multiplication Grade 4 — Chapter 1, Multiplying through 4 Digits by 1 Digit — 20

## Page 21

**Multiplying 3 Digits by 1 Digit** — SCORE /20

Multiply.

| | a | b | c | d | e |
|---|---|---|---|---|---|
| 1. | 137 ×5 = 685 | 129 ×9 = 1161 | 243 ×4 = 972 | 398 ×2 = 796 | 652 ×3 = 1956 |
| 2. | 142 ×4 = 568 | 704 ×8 = 5632 | 193 ×7 = 1351 | 246 ×3 = 738 | 152 ×7 = 1064 |
| 3. | 704 ×6 = 4224 | 751 ×3 = 2253 | 200 ×7 = 1400 | 555 ×2 = 1110 | 909 ×2 = 1818 |
| 4. | 730 ×7 = 5110 | 328 ×7 = 2296 | 462 ×6 = 2772 | 294 ×3 = 882 | 847 ×4 = 3388 |

Spectrum Multiplication Grade 4 — Chapter 1, Multiplying through 4 Digits by 1 Digit — 21

## Page 22

**Multiplication Practice** — SCORE /25

Multiply.

| | a | b | c | d | e |
|---|---|---|---|---|---|
| 1. | 416 ×4 = 1664 | 318 ×6 = 1908 | 379 ×2 = 758 | 719 ×9 = 6471 | 168 ×7 = 1176 |
| 2. | 713 ×8 = 5704 | 219 ×6 = 1314 | 237 ×5 = 1185 | 279 ×3 = 837 | 173 ×9 = 1557 |
| 3. | 164 ×6 = 984 | 179 ×8 = 1432 | 716 ×7 = 5012 | 298 ×4 = 1192 | 836 ×3 = 2508 |
| 4. | 632 ×5 = 3160 | 218 ×9 = 1962 | 816 ×8 = 6528 | 421 ×6 = 2526 | 248 ×2 = 496 |
| 5. | 541 ×7 = 3787 | 918 ×4 = 3672 | 641 ×9 = 5769 | 836 ×3 = 2508 | 941 ×8 = 7528 |

Spectrum Multiplication Grade 4 — Chapter 1, Multiplying through 4 Digits by 1 Digit — 22

# Answer Key

# Answer Key

## Page 29

NAME _____    SCORE ⬤ / 20

**Multiplication Practice**

Multiply.

| | a | b | c | d | e |
|---|---|---|---|---|---|
| 1. | 3243 × 6 = 19458 | 4254 × 7 = 29778 | 2435 × 9 = 21915 | 5201 × 5 = 26005 | 3643 × 8 = 29144 |
| 2. | 1476 × 4 = 5904 | 3629 × 5 = 18145 | 7642 × 7 = 53494 | 5624 × 4 = 22496 | 3928 × 8 = 31424 |
| 3. | 8215 × 6 = 49290 | 1826 × 9 = 16434 | 3214 × 8 = 25712 | 3265 × 4 = 13060 | 5429 × 5 = 27145 |
| 4. | 9267 × 3 = 27801 | 6254 × 7 = 43778 | 1242 × 8 = 9936 | 3263 × 6 = 19578 | 5584 × 2 = 11168 |

**29**

## Page 30

NAME _____    SCORE ⬤ / 20

**Multiplication Practice**

Multiply.

| | a | b | c | d | e |
|---|---|---|---|---|---|
| 1. | 6 × 3 = 18 | 8 × 2 = 16 | 4 × 7 = 28 | 22 × 9 = 198 | 17 × 6 = 102 |
| 2. | 74 × 6 = 444 | 34 × 9 = 306 | 28 × 6 = 168 | 163 × 1 = 163 | 317 × 4 = 1268 |
| 3. | 836 × 4 = 3344 | 627 × 8 = 5016 | 352 × 2 = 704 | 73 × 7 = 511 | 65 × 9 = 585 |
| 4. | 26 × 5 = 130 | 84 × 8 = 672 | 92 × 3 = 276 | 258 × 4 = 1032 | 736 × 8 = 5888 |

**30**

## Page 31

NAME _____

💡 **Check What You Learned**

Multiplying through 4 Digits by 1 Digit

Multiply.

| | a | b | c | d | e |
|---|---|---|---|---|---|
| 1. | 26 × 3 = 78 | 24 × 4 = 96 | 647 × 2 = 1294 | 14 × 6 = 84 | 9353 × 4 = 37412 |
| 2. | 739 × 2 = 1478 | 4 × 7 = 28 | 25 × 3 = 75 | 5613 × 5 = 28065 | 37 × 2 = 74 |
| 3. | 48 × 2 = 96 | 4623 × 4 = 18492 | 935 × 2 = 1870 | 12 × 8 = 96 | 1324 × 3 = 3972 |
| 4. | 9413 × 6 = 56478 | 818 × 5 = 4090 | 29 × 3 = 87 | 7 × 5 = 35 | 49 × 2 = 98 |
| 5. | 6 × 6 = 36 | 36 × 2 = 72 | 2818 × 3 = 8454 | 415 × 6 = 2490 | 27 × 3 = 81 |
| 6. | 213 × 7 = 1491 | 28 × 3 = 84 | 9 × 5 = 45 | 46 × 2 = 92 | 816 × 5 = 4080 |

CHAPTER 1 POSTTEST

**31**

## Page 32

NAME _____

CHAPTER 2 PRETEST

🔍 **Check What You Know**

Problem Solving: Multiplying through 4 Digits by 1 Digit

Read the problem carefully and solve. Show your work under each question.

Sue's Supply Shop places an order for more office supplies. Sue orders 9 boxes of blue pens. Thirty-five pens come in each box. Paperclips come in boxes of 1,165, and she orders 7 boxes. She also orders 8 boxes of rulers, and 15 rulers come in each box.

1. Sue plans to have a sale on blue pens. How many blue pens does Sue order in total?

___315___ blue pens

2. How many total paperclips does Sue order?

___8155___ paperclips

3. Sue wants to make sure she has enough space on her shelves for all the rulers she orders. How many rulers altogether does she order?

___120___ rulers

4. When Sue receives the order, she finds that 5 of the 9 pen boxes are filled with black pens instead of blue pens. How many blue pens does Sue have from the order?

___140___ blue pens

**32**

## Page 33

NAME _____    SCORE ⬤ / 3

**Multiplying Single Digits**

Read the problem carefully and solve. Show your work under each question.

Ella makes necklaces for a craft fair. For each necklace, she uses 4 yellow beads, 7 blue beads, 6 red beads, and 8 green beads.

> **Helpful Hint**
> To solve a multiplication word problem, you need to find:
> 1. the number of groups
> 2. the number of items in each group

1. Ella makes 9 necklaces. How many green beads does she use?

___72___ green beads

2. How many yellow beads does Ella use to make 9 necklaces?

___36___ yellow beads

3. To make 6 necklaces, how many red beads does Ella use? Write the corresponding addition problem.

__6 + 6 + 6 + 6 + 6 + 6 = 36__ red beads

**33**

## Page 34

NAME _____    SCORE ⬤ / 3

**Multiplying 2 Digits by 1 Digit**

Read the problem carefully and solve. Show your work under each question.

Roger and his friend Aaron like to go mountain biking. They keep track of the total miles they bike each week. Roger bikes 32 miles each week. Aaron bikes 23 miles each week.

> **Helpful Hint**
> To find the answer or product:
> 1. Multiply 3 ones by 2.
> 2. Then, multiply 2 tens by 2.
> 23 × 2 = 46

1. After 3 weeks, how many miles has Roger biked in total?

___96___ miles

2. Aaron calculates the total number of miles he biked in 3 weeks. How many miles did he bike?

___69___ miles

3. Roger biked an extra mile each week for 3 weeks. How many total miles did he bike during those 3 weeks?

___99___ miles

**34**

## Page 35

**Multiplying 2 Digits by 1 Digit**

Solve each problem. Show your work under each question.

**Helpful Hint**

If you know the total number of items in a group and the number of groups, then you can write an equation to help you solve the problem using multiplication:

8 x a = 96

8 x 12 = 96

a = 12

1. There are 48 chicken farms near an Ohio town. If each farm has 9 barns, how many total barns are there?

There are __432__ total barns.

2. Mr. Ferris has a canoe rental business. Over the weekend, he rented 47 canoes. A canoe holds 3 people. If each canoe was full, how many people did Mr. Ferris rent to over the weekend?

Mr. Ferris rented to __141__ people.

3. The school bought 368 slices of pizza to serve at the school dance. If the school planned for each student to have 4 slices of pizza, how many students will attend the dance? Write a multiplication equation to find how many students will attend the dance. Then, solve.

4 x a = 368     __92__ students will attend the dance.

Spectrum Multiplication
Grade 4
Problem Solving: Multiplying through 4 Digits by 1 Digit     Chapter 2     35

**35**

## Page 36

**Multiplying 2 Digits by 1 Digit**

Solve each problem. Show your work under each question.

1. The pool opened on Memorial Day. Ninety-four people showed up. The pool manager gave out 2 vouchers to each person for free drinks. How many vouchers did the pool manager give out?

The manager gave out __188__ vouchers.

2. In the Sumton community, there are 56 houses. If there are 3 children living in each house, how many children live in houses in Sumton?

There are __168__ children living in houses in Sumton.

3. Deon and Denise need 115 dollars to buy a computer game. If they save the same amount of money each week for 5 weeks, how much money will they need to save each week? Write a multiplication equation to find how much Deon and Denise need to save each week. Then, solve.

5 x a = 115     __23__ dollars

Spectrum Multiplication
Grade 4
Problem Solving: Multiplying through 4 Digits by 1 Digit     Chapter 2     36

**36**

## Page 37

**Multiplying 2 Digits by 1 Digit**

Solve each problem. Show your work under each question.

1. Mr. Benson must order 32 calculators for each fifth grade class. There are 6 classes. How many calculators must Mr. Benson order?

Each class needs __32__ calculators.

There are __6__ classes.

Mr. Benson must order __192__ calculators.

2. It takes Rosa 73 minutes to knit a scarf. How many minutes will it take her to knit 4 scarves?

It will take Rosa __73__ minutes to knit a scarf.

She wants to knit __4__ scarves.

It will take Rosa __292__ minutes.

Spectrum Multiplication
Grade 4
Problem Solving: Multiplying through 4 Digits by 1 Digit     Chapter 2     37

**37**

## Page 38

**Multiplying 3 Digits by 1 Digit**

Read the problem carefully and solve. Show your work under each question.

A computer game company held a contest on Saturday. The company kept track of how many hours each person participated in the contest. 327 people played for 2 hours. 113 people played for 3 hours. 373 people played for 4 hours. 235 people played for 5 hours. 118 people played for 6 hours.

**Helpful Hint**

To find the total time a group of people spends on an activity, multiply the number of people by the time each one spends on the activity.

1. Which group of people played the most number of hours? How many total hours did they play?

the group of __373__ people

__1492__ hours

2. Some of the participants played in the contest for 6 hours. How many total hours did these participants play?

__708__ hours

Spectrum Multiplication
Grade 4
Problem Solving: Multiplying through 4 Digits by 1 Digit     Chapter 2     38

**38**

## Page 39

**Multiplying 3 Digits by 1 Digit**

3. How many total hours did the group with 113 participants play in the contest?

__339__ hours

4. One group of participants played for the shortest amount of time. How many total hours did this group play?

__654__ hours

5. How many total hours did the group with 235 participants play in the contest?

__1175__ hours

Spectrum Multiplication
Grade 4
Problem Solving: Multiplying through 4 Digits by 1 Digit     Chapter 2     39

**39**

## Page 40

**Multiplying 4 Digits by 1 Digit**

Read the problem carefully and solve. Show your work under each question.

Jerome loves to help take care of the crops on his grandfather's farm. There are 8 rows of tomato plants with 1,209 plants in each row. The carrots are planted in 9 rows with 47 plants in each row. There are also 7 rows of pepper plants with 106 plants in each row.

**Helpful Hint**

When multiplying a number with zeros in it, remember to multiply and rename the places correctly:

$$\begin{array}{r} 2\overset{3}{0}8 \\ \times \quad 4 \\ \hline 832 \end{array}$$

1. How many pepper plants are there in all? How many carrot plants are there in all?

__742__ pepper plants

__423__ carrot plants

2. Jerome loves tomatoes. What is the total number of tomato plants at the farm?

__9672__ tomato plants

3. Jerome's grandfather wants to add 3 more rows of pepper plants. What is the total number of pepper plants he will add to his crop?

__318__ pepper plants

Spectrum Multiplication
Grade 4
Problem Solving: Multiplying through 4 Digits by 1 Digit     Chapter 2     40

**40**

# Answer Key

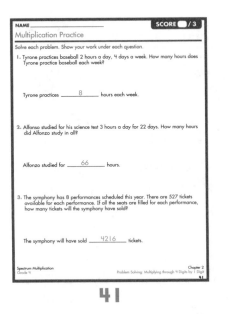
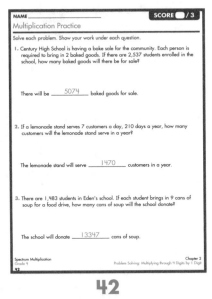
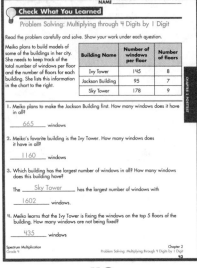
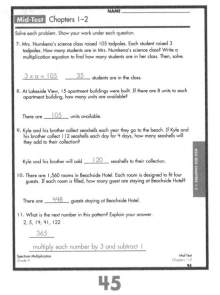

# Answer Key

---

## Multiplying 2 Digits by 2 Digits

Multiply 9 ones by 7.
19
×27
133

19
×27
133
Put 6 tens above the 1.
Multiply 1 ten by 7.
Then, add 6 tens.

19
×27
133
38
Multiply 9 ones by 2.
Put 1 ten above the 1.
Multiply 1 ten by 2.
Then, add 1 ten.

19
× 27
133
+380
513
Add.

Multiply.

| | a | b | c | d | e | f |
|---|---|---|---|---|---|---|
| 1. | 22 ×33 = 726 | 11 ×45 = 495 | 80 ×10 = 800 | 31 ×23 = 713 | 13 ×12 = 156 | 30 ×31 = 930 |
| 2. | 41 ×21 = 861 | 32 ×20 = 640 | 40 ×10 = 400 | 21 ×31 = 651 | 30 ×30 = 900 | 14 ×10 = 140 |
| 3. | 22 ×44 = 968 | 14 ×20 = 280 | 40 ×12 = 480 | 90 ×10 = 900 | 13 ×13 = 169 | 30 ×11 = 330 |

Spectrum Multiplication
Grade 4
Chapter 3
Multiplying through 3 Digits by 2 Digits
47

**47**

---

## Multiplying 2 Digits by 2 Digits

Multiply.

| | a | b | c | d | e | f |
|---|---|---|---|---|---|---|
| 1. | 22 ×19 = 418 | 32 ×41 = 1312 | 72 ×18 = 1296 | 45 ×15 = 675 | 48 ×20 = 960 | 77 ×22 = 1694 |
| 2. | 63 ×24 = 1512 | 52 ×48 = 2496 | 28 ×25 = 700 | 77 ×30 = 2310 | 33 ×29 = 957 | 90 ×70 = 6300 |
| 3. | 57 ×23 = 1311 | 18 ×18 = 324 | 77 ×27 = 2079 | 65 ×17 = 1105 | 88 ×22 = 1936 | 90 ×20 = 1800 |
| 4. | 37 ×23 = 851 | 91 ×38 = 3458 | 44 ×43 = 1892 | 17 ×13 = 221 | 88 ×17 = 1496 | 55 ×38 = 2090 |

Spectrum Multiplication
Grade 4
Chapter 3
Multiplying through 3 Digits by 2 Digits
48

**48**

---

## Multiplication Practice

Multiply.

| | a | b | c | d | e | f |
|---|---|---|---|---|---|---|
| 1. | 45 ×23 = 1035 | 53 ×17 = 901 | 25 ×47 = 1175 | 48 ×34 = 1632 | 54 ×23 = 1242 | 32 ×51 = 1632 |
| 2. | 35 ×63 = 2205 | 44 ×29 = 1276 | 58 ×37 = 2146 | 39 ×14 = 546 | 62 ×46 = 2852 | 36 ×52 = 1872 |
| 3. | 57 ×32 = 1824 | 49 ×27 = 1323 | 24 ×68 = 1632 | 37 ×43 = 1591 | 71 ×54 = 3834 | 35 ×42 = 1470 |
| 4. | 56 ×23 = 1288 | 39 ×32 = 1248 | 23 ×64 = 1472 | 43 ×35 = 1505 | 37 ×19 = 703 | 42 ×37 = 1554 |

Spectrum Multiplication
Grade 4
Chapter 3
Multiplying through 3 Digits by 2 Digits
49

**49**

---

## Multiplication Practice

Multiply.

| | a | b | c | d | e | f |
|---|---|---|---|---|---|---|
| 1. | 45 ×38 = 1710 | 28 ×57 = 1596 | 47 ×63 = 2961 | 36 ×82 = 2952 | 53 ×74 = 3922 | 63 ×28 = 1764 |
| 2. | 39 ×45 = 1755 | 84 ×53 = 4452 | 28 ×39 = 1092 | 65 ×83 = 5395 | 48 ×63 = 3024 | 67 ×25 = 1675 |
| 3. | 27 ×49 = 1323 | 82 ×36 = 2952 | 24 ×93 = 2232 | 48 ×30 = 1440 | 83 ×62 = 5146 | 46 ×81 = 3726 |
| 4. | 57 ×38 = 2166 | 62 ×54 = 3348 | 76 ×46 = 3496 | 49 ×73 = 3577 | 54 ×18 = 972 | 74 ×36 = 2664 |

Spectrum Multiplication
Grade 4
Chapter 3
Multiplying through 3 Digits by 2 Digits
50

**50**

---

## Multiplication Practice

Multiply.

| | a | b | c | d |
|---|---|---|---|---|
| 1. | 45 ×27 = 1215 | 62 ×39 = 2418 | 28 ×45 = 1260 | 76 ×66 = 5016 |
| 2. | 25 ×13 = 325 | 59 ×32 = 1888 | 80 ×93 = 7440 | 14 ×37 = 518 |
| 3. | 97 ×48 = 4656 | 92 ×82 = 7544 | 58 ×32 = 1856 | 91 ×54 = 4914 |
| 4. | 12 ×61 = 732 | 94 ×27 = 2538 | 75 ×69 = 5175 | 50 ×37 = 1850 |
| 5. | 76 ×83 = 6308 | 92 ×62 = 5704 | 15 ×41 = 615 | 39 ×74 = 2886 |

Spectrum Multiplication
Grade 4
Chapter 3
Multiplying through 3 Digits by 2 Digits
51

**51**

---

## Multiplication Practice

Multiply.

| | a | b | c | d | e |
|---|---|---|---|---|---|
| 1. | 78 ×39 = 3042 | 56 ×28 = 1568 | 97 ×59 = 5723 | 48 ×78 = 3744 | 25 ×49 = 1225 |
| 2. | 98 ×98 = 9604 | 78 ×15 = 1170 | 48 ×36 = 1728 | 77 ×54 = 4158 | 83 ×27 = 2241 |
| 3. | 70 ×36 = 2520 | 89 ×18 = 1602 | 15 ×48 = 720 | 47 ×32 = 1504 | 50 ×78 = 3900 |
| 4. | 35 ×42 = 1470 | 20 ×42 = 840 | 72 ×68 = 4896 | 59 ×24 = 1416 | 24 ×50 = 1200 |

Spectrum Multiplication
Grade 4
Chapter 3
Multiplying through 3 Digits by 2 Digits
52

**52**

---

Spectrum Multiplication
Grade 4

Answer Key

**91**

## 53

**Multiplication Practice**

Multiply.

| | a | b | c | d | e |
|---|---|---|---|---|---|
| 1. | 315 ×30 = 9450 | 527 ×42 = 22134 | 287 ×21 = 6027 | 242 ×70 = 16940 | 209 ×30 = 6270 |
| 2. | 140 ×32 = 4480 | 196 ×23 = 4508 | 673 ×92 = 61916 | 542 ×48 = 26016 | 604 ×40 = 24160 |
| 3. | 713 ×67 = 47771 | 900 ×42 = 37800 | 198 ×72 = 14256 | 513 ×58 = 29754 | 841 ×71 = 59711 |
| 4. | 125 ×73 = 9125 | 706 ×31 = 21886 | 448 ×33 = 14784 | 809 ×12 = 9708 | 615 ×73 = 44895 |

## 54

**Multiplication Practice**

Multiply.

| | a | b | c | d | e |
|---|---|---|---|---|---|
| 1. | 326 ×14 = 4564 | 345 ×23 = 7935 | 265 ×13 = 3445 | 416 ×25 = 10400 | 364 ×18 = 6552 |
| 2. | 516 ×32 = 16512 | 365 ×41 = 14965 | 423 ×51 = 21573 | 363 ×23 = 8349 | 245 ×34 = 8330 |
| 3. | 523 ×15 = 7845 | 142 ×28 = 3976 | 212 ×45 = 9540 | 234 ×36 = 8424 | 325 ×24 = 7800 |
| 4. | 232 ×19 = 4408 | 425 ×43 = 22575 | 443 ×24 = 10632 | 312 ×52 = 16224 | 286 ×34 = 9724 |

## 55

**Multiplication Practice**

Multiply.

| | a | b | c | d | e |
|---|---|---|---|---|---|
| 1. | 407 ×39 = 15873 | 530 ×62 = 32860 | 261 ×40 = 10440 | 704 ×82 = 57728 | 607 ×53 = 32171 |
| 2. | 437 ×20 = 8740 | 623 ×30 = 18690 | 140 ×57 = 7980 | 210 ×78 = 16380 | 527 ×30 = 15810 |
| 3. | 708 ×23 = 16284 | 283 ×40 = 11320 | 340 ×68 = 23120 | 630 ×24 = 15120 | 208 ×40 = 8320 |
| 4. | 896 ×30 = 26880 | 730 ×52 = 37960 | 347 ×80 = 27760 | 310 ×64 = 19840 | 488 ×20 = 9760 |

## 56

**Multiplication Practice**

Multiply.

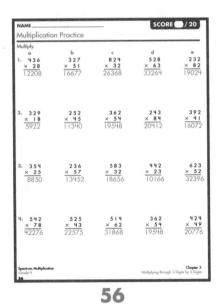

| | a | b | c | d | e |
|---|---|---|---|---|---|
| 1. | 436 ×28 = 12208 | 327 ×51 = 16677 | 824 ×32 = 26368 | 528 ×63 = 33264 | 232 ×82 = 19024 |
| 2. | 329 ×18 = 5922 | 252 ×45 = 11340 | 362 ×54 = 19548 | 243 ×84 = 20412 | 392 ×41 = 16072 |
| 3. | 354 ×25 = 8850 | 236 ×57 = 13452 | 583 ×32 = 18656 | 442 ×23 = 10166 | 623 ×52 = 32396 |
| 4. | 542 ×78 = 42276 | 525 ×43 = 22575 | 514 ×62 = 31868 | 362 ×54 = 19548 | 424 ×49 = 20776 |

## 57

**Multiplication Practice**

Multiply.

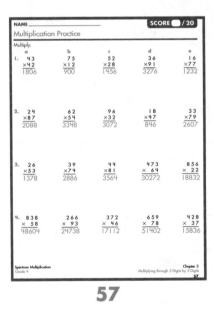

| | a | b | c | d | e |
|---|---|---|---|---|---|
| 1. | 43 ×42 = 1806 | 75 ×12 = 900 | 52 ×28 = 1456 | 36 ×91 = 3276 | 16 ×77 = 1232 |
| 2. | 24 ×87 = 2088 | 62 ×54 = 3348 | 96 ×32 = 3072 | 18 ×47 = 846 | 33 ×79 = 2607 |
| 3. | 26 ×53 = 1378 | 39 ×74 = 2886 | 44 ×81 = 3564 | 473 ×64 = 30272 | 856 ×22 = 18832 |
| 4. | 838 ×58 = 48604 | 266 ×93 = 24738 | 372 ×46 = 17112 | 659 ×78 = 51402 | 428 ×37 = 15836 |

## 58

**Multiplication Practice**

Multiply.

| | a | b | c | d | e |
|---|---|---|---|---|---|
| 1. | 28 ×24 = 672 | 35 ×18 = 630 | 26 ×33 = 858 | 85 ×45 = 3825 | 43 ×62 = 2666 |
| 2. | 482 ×26 = 12532 | 49 ×54 = 2646 | 263 ×84 = 22092 | 132 ×68 = 8976 | 164 ×42 = 6888 |
| 3. | 324 ×27 = 8748 | 816 ×16 = 13056 | 255 ×44 = 11220 | 165 ×23 = 3795 | 66 ×71 = 4686 |
| 4. | 150 ×22 = 3300 | 182 ×12 = 2184 | 324 ×36 = 11664 | 522 ×63 = 32886 | 38 ×24 = 912 |

# Answer Key

## Page 59 — Multiplication Practice  SCORE /25

Multiply.

| | a | b | c | d | e |
|---|---|---|---|---|---|
| 1. | 627 × 28 = 17556 | 205 × 67 = 13735 | 364 × 42 = 15288 | 423 × 57 = 24111 | 920 × 84 = 77280 |
| 2. | 549 × 30 = 16470 | 847 × 27 = 22869 | 925 × 56 = 51800 | 427 × 93 = 39711 | 240 × 64 = 15360 |
| 3. | 149 × 80 = 11920 | 847 × 92 = 77924 | 148 × 24 = 3552 | 492 × 76 = 37392 | 284 × 33 = 9372 |
| 4. | 620 × 34 = 21080 | 413 × 47 = 19411 | 404 × 76 = 30704 | 243 × 91 = 22113 | 128 × 24 = 3072 |
| 5. | 136 × 58 = 7888 | 132 × 49 = 6468 | 149 × 26 = 3874 | 427 × 78 = 33306 | 264 × 32 = 8448 |

Spectrum Multiplication  Grade 4  — Chapter 3 — Multiplying through 3 Digits by 2 Digits — 59

**59**

## Page 60 — Multiplication Practice  SCORE /20

Multiply.

| | a | b | c | d | e |
|---|---|---|---|---|---|
| 1. | 24 ×75 = 1800 | 936 × 47 = 43992 | 365 × 28 = 10220 | 573 × 65 = 37245 | 92 ×84 = 7728 |
| 2. | 476 × 83 = 39508 | 468 × 57 = 26676 | 23 ×92 = 2116 | 645 × 73 = 47085 | 765 × 48 = 36720 |
| 3. | 59 ×63 = 3717 | 368 × 87 = 32016 | 28 ×61 = 1708 | 537 × 44 = 23628 | 804 × 87 = 69948 |
| 4. | 48 ×29 = 1392 | 37 ×73 = 2701 | 725 × 52 = 37700 | 39 ×38 = 1482 | 457 × 86 = 39302 |

Spectrum Multiplication  Grade 4  — Chapter 3 — Multiplying through 3 Digits by 2 Digits — 60

**60**

## Page 61 — Multiplication Practice  SCORE /20

Multiply.

| | a | b | c | d | e |
|---|---|---|---|---|---|
| 1. | 467 × 35 = 16345 | 538 × 47 = 25286 | 393 × 82 = 32226 | 724 × 56 = 40544 | 821 × 75 = 61575 |
| 2. | 463 × 43 = 19909 | 522 × 68 = 35496 | 326 × 92 = 29992 | 735 × 45 = 33075 | 268 × 39 = 10452 |
| 3. | 534 × 76 = 40584 | 232 × 98 = 22736 | 845 × 63 = 53235 | 928 × 81 = 75168 | 625 × 33 = 20625 |
| 4. | 856 × 42 = 35952 | 932 × 58 = 54056 | 734 × 54 = 39636 | 487 × 72 = 35064 | 289 × 79 = 22831 |

Spectrum Multiplication  Grade 4  — Chapter 3 — Multiplying through 3 Digits by 2 Digits — 61

**61**

## Page 62 — Estimating Products  SCORE /20

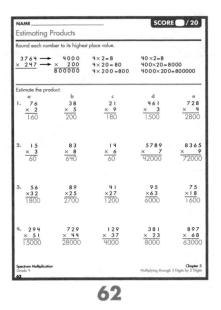

Round each number to its highest place value.

$$3764 \rightarrow 4000$$
$$\times 247 \rightarrow \times 200$$
$$800000$$

| $4 \times 2 = 8$ | $40 \times 2 = 8$ |
|---|---|
| $4 \times 20 = 80$ | $400 \times 20 = 8000$ |
| $4 \times 200 = 800$ | $4000 \times 200 = 800000$ |

Estimate the product.

| | a | b | c | d | e |
|---|---|---|---|---|---|
| 1. | 76 × 2 = 160 | 38 × 5 = 200 | 21 × 9 = 180 | 461 × 3 = 1500 | 728 × 4 = 2800 |
| 2. | 15 × 3 = 60 | 83 × 8 = 640 | 14 × 6 = 60 | 5789 × 7 = 42000 | 8365 × 9 = 72000 |
| 3. | 56 ×32 = 1800 | 89 ×25 = 2700 | 41 ×27 = 1200 | 95 ×63 = 6000 | 75 ×18 = 1600 |
| 4. | 294 × 51 = 15000 | 729 × 44 = 28000 | 129 × 23 = 4000 | 381 × 23 = 8000 | 897 × 68 = 63000 |

Spectrum Multiplication  Grade 4  — Chapter 3 — Multiplying through 3 Digits by 2 Digits — 62

**62**

## Page 63 — Check What You Learned

Multiplying through 3 Digits by 2 Digits

Multiply.

| | a | b | c | d | e | f | g |
|---|---|---|---|---|---|---|---|
| 1. | 72 ×14 = 1008 | 24 ×68 = 1632 | 339 × 42 = 14238 | 34 × 28 = 952 | 150 × 19 = 2850 | 333 × 22 = 7326 | 93 ×42 = 3906 |
| 2. | 42 ×62 = 2604 | 64 ×18 = 1152 | 31 ×27 = 837 | 300 × 21 = 6300 | 72 ×94 = 6768 | 73 ×28 = 2044 | 28 ×28 = 2520 |
| 3. | 81 ×76 = 6156 | 728 × 61 = 44408 | 22 ×43 = 946 | 207 × 21 = 4347 | 90 ×56 = 5040 | 79 ×44 = 3476 | 643 × 37 = 23791 |
| 4. | 743 × 12 = 8916 | 439 × 10 = 4390 | 117 × 23 = 2691 | 43 ×46 = 1978 | 84 ×65 = 5460 | 20 ×19 = 380 | 555 × 40 = 22200 |
| 5. | 42 ×41 = 1722 | 311 × 12 = 3732 | 72 ×18 = 1296 | 12 ×11 = 132 | 50 ×42 = 2100 | 95 ×27 = 2565 | 353 × 17 = 6001 |
| 6. | 606 × 12 = 7272 | 786 × 31 = 24366 | 202 × 33 = 6666 | 52 ×49 = 2548 | 86 ×14 = 1204 | 94 ×65 = 6110 | 403 × 55 = 22165 |

CHAPTER 3 POSTTEST

Spectrum Multiplication  Grade 4  — Chapter 3 — Multiplying through 3 Digits by 2 Digits — 63

**63**

## Page 64 — Check What You Know

Problem Solving: Multiplying through 3 Digits by 2 Digits

CHAPTER 4 PRETEST

Read the problem carefully and solve. Show your work under each question.

Students in Thorton's schools are collecting soda cans and bottles for a charity drive. They have a contest to see which students and which schools collect the most cans and bottles.

1. Elmhurst has 328 students. Each student collects 28 cans during the contest. How many cans do the students collect altogether?

   _9184_ cans

2. At Oakwood, 47 students collect 125 bottles each. How many bottles do the students collect in all?

   _5875_ bottles

3. Park Central has 156 students. Each student collects 14 bottles. How many bottles do they collect in total?

   _2184_ bottles

4. The contest lasts 15 weeks. One student, Raul, collects 33 cans per week. How many cans does Raul collect during the contest?

   _495_ cans

Spectrum Multiplication  Grade 4  — Chapter 4 — Problem Solving: Multiplying through 3 Digits by 2 Digits — 64

**64**

---

## Multiplying 2 Digits by 2 Digits

Read the problem carefully and solve. Show your work under each question.

Olivia's Orchards grows two types of apples. One type is red and the other is green. The trees that grow red apples are planted in 34 rows with 68 trees in each row. The trees that grow green apples are planted in 26 rows with 47 trees in each row.

**Helpful Hint**
Remember to add a zero at the end of the second product to show that you are multiplying 31 by 2 tens:

$$\begin{array}{r} 31 \\ \times\ 23 \\ \hline 93 \\ +620 \\ \hline 713 \end{array}$$

1. How many of the trees in the orchard grow red apples?

___2312___ trees

2. What is the total number of trees in the orchard that grow green apples?

___1222___ trees

3. The orchard decides to rope off three rows of red apple trees for a school group to go apple picking. How many red apple trees are not roped off?

___2108___ red apple trees

Spectrum Multiplication
Grade 4
Problem Solving: Multiplying through 3 Digits by 2 Digits
65

### 65

---

## Multiplying 2 Digits by 2 Digits

Read the problem carefully and solve. Show your work under each question.

Ramon's fourth grade class performs a play for their parents. Ramon and other students help set up chairs for the performance. They set up 13 rows of chairs and each row has 21 chairs.

1. How many chairs did the students set up?

___273___ chairs

2. The third grade classes are invited to watch. Two rows of chairs are saved for them. How many chairs are left for the parents to use?

___231___ chairs

3. Before the play starts, the principal decides to add 2 more chairs to each row. How many total chairs are there now?

___299___ chairs

Spectrum Multiplication
Grade 4
Problem Solving: Multiplying through 3 Digits by 2 Digits
66

### 66

---

## Multiplying 2 Digits by 2 Digits

Solve each problem. Show your work under each question.

1. There are 24 hours in one day. How many hours are there in 18 days?

There are ___24___ hours in a day.

There are ___432___ hours in 18 days.

2. It takes 47 apples to fill a bushel. There are 24 bushels to fill. How many apples does the farmer need to fill all the bushels?

There are ___47___ apples in a bushel.

There are ___24___ bushels to fill.

The farmer needs ___1128___ apples to fill all the bushels.

3. Bob's car can go 23 miles on one gallon of gas. The gas tank holds 26 gallons. How many miles can Bob's car go on a full tank of gas?

Bob's car can go ___23___ miles on one gallon.

The car holds ___26___ gallons of gas.

It can go ___598___ miles on a full tank of gas.

Spectrum Multiplication
Grade 4
Problem Solving: Multiplying through 3 Digits by 2 Digits
67

### 67

---

## Multiplying 2 Digits by 2 Digits

Solve each problem. Show your work under each question.

1. Buses were reserved for a field trip. If each bus holds 20 students, how many students would 16 buses hold?

The buses would hold ___320___ students.

2. If 16 potato chips is a serving size and there are 15 servings in a bag, how many potato chips are in each bag?

There are ___240___ chips in a bag.

3. There are 48 cabins at summer camp. If each cabin holds 25 campers, how many campers are at summer camp?

There are ___1200___ campers at summer camp.

Spectrum Multiplication
Grade 4
Problem Solving: Multiplying through 3 Digits by 2 Digits
68

### 68

---

## Multiplying 2 Digits by 2 Digits

Solve each problem. Show your work under each question.

1. On Monday, the amusement park offered tickets for 10 dollars. In the first hour, 96 people bought tickets for the park. How much money did the park make on ticket sales in the first hour?

The amusement park made ___960___ dollars in the first hour.

2. Mr. Tao taught mathematics to classes of 37 students for 27 years. How many students has Mr. Tao taught in all?

Mr. Tao has taught ___999___ students.

3. If Latisha brushes her teeth 14 times a week, how many times will Latisha have brushed her teeth in 72 weeks?

Latisha will have brushed her teeth ___1008___ times.

Spectrum Multiplication
Grade 4
Problem Solving: Multiplying through 3 Digits by 2 Digits
69

### 69

---

## Multiplying 3 Digits by 2 Digits

Read the problem carefully and solve. Show your work under each question.

Meiko researches the buildings in her city. The tallest building has 43 floors and 219 windows on each floor. Meiko's father, Mr. Arimoto, works in the building across the street. His building has 27 floors and 128 windows on each floor.

1. How many total windows does the tallest building have?

___9417___ windows

2. How many total windows does the building Mr. Arimoto works in have?

___3456___ windows

3. Window washers washed the windows on 8 floors of Mr. Arimoto's building. How many windows do they have left to wash?

___2432___ windows

Spectrum Multiplication
Grade 4
Problem Solving: Multiplying through 3 Digits by 2 Digits
70

### 70

---

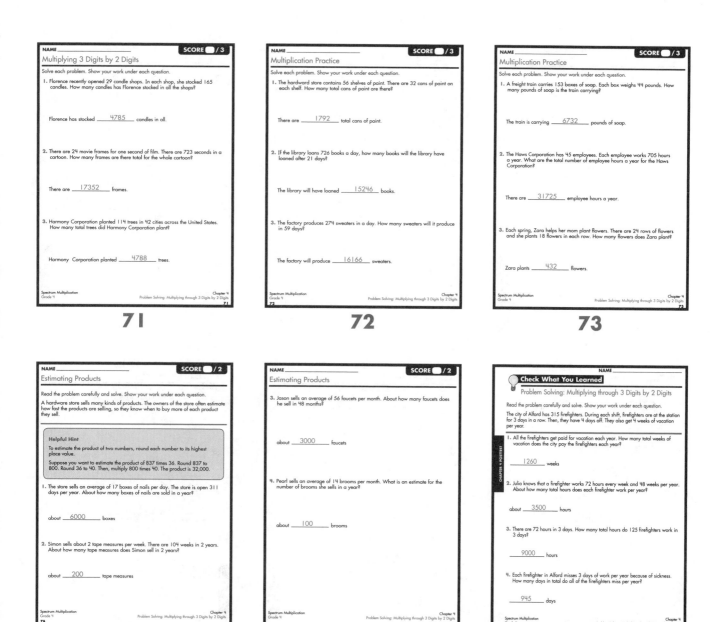

**71**

### Multiplying 3 Digits by 2 Digits
SCORE /3

Solve each problem. Show your work under each question.

1. Florence recently opened 29 candle shops. In each shop, she stocked 165 candles. How many candles has Florence stocked in all the shops?

Florence has stocked ___4785___ candles in all.

2. There are 24 movie frames for one second of film. There are 723 seconds in a cartoon. How many frames are there total for the whole cartoon?

There are ___17352___ frames.

3. Harmony Corporation planted 114 trees in 42 cities across the United States. How many total trees did Harmony Corporation plant?

Harmony Corporation planted ___4788___ trees.

**72**

### Multiplication Practice
SCORE /3

Solve each problem. Show your work under each question.

1. The hardware store contains 56 shelves of paint. There are 32 cans of paint on each shelf. How many total cans of paint are there?

There are ___1792___ total cans of paint.

2. If the library loans 726 books a day, how many books will the library have loaned after 21 days?

The library will have loaned ___15246___ books.

3. The factory produces 274 sweaters in a day. How many sweaters will it produce in 59 days?

The factory will produce ___16166___ sweaters.

**73**

### Multiplication Practice
SCORE /3

Solve each problem. Show your work under each question.

1. A freight train carries 153 boxes of soap. Each box weighs 44 pounds. How many pounds of soap is the train carrying?

The train is carrying ___6732___ pounds of soap.

2. The Haws Corporation has 45 employees. Each employee works 705 hours a year. What are the total number of employee hours a year for the Haws Corporation?

There are ___31725___ employee hours a year.

3. Each spring, Zara helps her mom plant flowers. There are 24 rows of flowers and she plants 18 flowers in each row. How many flowers does Zara plant?

Zara plants ___432___ flowers.

**74**

### Estimating Products
SCORE /2

Read the problem carefully and solve. Show your work under each question.

A hardware store sells many kinds of products. The owners of the store often estimate how fast the products are selling, so they know when to buy more of each product they sell.

**Helpful Hint**
To estimate the product of two numbers, round each number to its highest place value.
Suppose you want to estimate the product of 837 times 36. Round 837 to 800. Round 36 to 40. Then, multiply 800 times 40. The product is 32,000.

1. The store sells an average of 17 boxes of nails per day. The store is open 311 days per year. About how many boxes of nails are sold in a year?

about ___6000___ boxes

2. Simon sells about 2 tape measures per week. There are 104 weeks in 2 years. About how many tape measures does Simon sell in 2 years?

about ___200___ tape measures

**75**

### Estimating Products
SCORE /2

3. Jason sells an average of 56 faucets per month. About how many faucets does he sell in 48 months?

about ___3000___ faucets

4. Pearl sells an average of 14 brooms per month. What is an estimate for the number of brooms she sells in a year?

about ___100___ brooms

**76**

### Check What You Learned
Problem Solving: Multiplying through 3 Digits by 2 Digits

Read the problem carefully and solve. Show your work under each question.

The city of Alford has 315 firefighters. During each shift, firefighters are at the station for 3 days in a row. Then, they have 4 days off. They also get 4 weeks of vacation per year.

1. All the firefighters get paid for vacation each year. How many total weeks of vacation does the city pay the firefighters each year?

___1260___ weeks

2. Julia knows that a firefighter works 72 hours every week and 48 weeks per year. About how many total hours does each firefighter work per year?

about ___3500___ hours

3. There are 72 hours in 3 days. How many total hours do 125 firefighters work in 3 days?

___9000___ hours

4. Each firefighter in Alford misses 3 days of work per year because of sickness. How many days in total do all of the firefighters miss per year?

___945___ days

# Answer Key

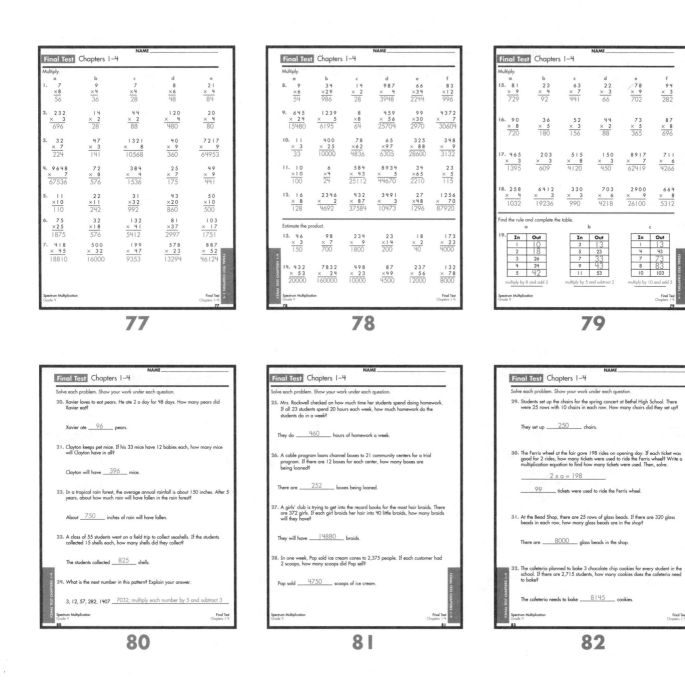

**77**

Final Test Chapters 1–4

Multiply.

| | a | b | c | d | e |
|---|---|---|---|---|---|
| 1. | 7 ×8 = 56 | 9 ×4 = 36 | 7 ×4 = 28 | 8 ×6 = 48 | 21 × 4 = 84 |
| 2. | 232 × 3 = 696 | 14 × 2 = 28 | 44 × 2 = 88 | 120 × 4 = 480 | 20 × 4 = 80 |
| 3. | 32 × 7 = 224 | 47 × 3 = 141 | 1321 × 8 = 10568 | 40 × 9 = 360 | 7217 × 9 = 64953 |
| 4. | 9648 × 7 = 67536 | 72 × 8 = 576 | 384 × 4 = 1536 | 25 × 7 = 175 | 49 × 9 = 441 |
| 5. | 11 ×10 = 110 | 22 ×11 = 242 | 31 ×32 = 992 | 43 ×20 = 860 | 50 ×10 = 500 |
| 6. | 75 ×25 = 1875 | 32 ×18 = 576 | 132 × 41 = 5412 | 81 ×37 = 2997 | 103 × 17 = 1751 |
| 7. | 418 × 45 = 18810 | 500 × 32 = 16000 | 199 × 47 = 9353 | 578 × 23 = 13294 | 887 × 52 = 46124 |

Spectrum Multiplication
Grade 4

Final Test
Chapters 1–4
77

**78**

Final Test Chapters 1–4

Multiply.

| | a | b | c | d | e | f |
|---|---|---|---|---|---|---|
| 8. | 9 ×6 = 54 | 34 ×29 = 986 | 14 × 2 = 28 | 987 × 4 = 3948 | 66 ×34 = 2244 | 83 ×12 = 996 |
| 9. | 645 × 24 = 15480 | 1239 × 5 = 6195 | 8 ×8 = 64 | 459 × 56 = 25704 | 99 ×30 = 2970 | 4372 × 7 = 30604 |
| 10. | 11 × 3 = 33 | 400 × 25 = 10000 | 78 ×62 = 4836 | 65 ×97 = 6305 | 325 × 88 = 28600 | 348 × 9 = 3132 |
| 11. | 10 ×10 = 100 | 6 ×4 = 24 | 584 × 43 = 25112 | 8934 × 5 = 44670 | 34 ×65 = 2210 | 23 × 5 = 115 |
| 12. | 16 × 8 = 128 | 2346 × 2 = 4692 | 432 ×87 = 37584 | 3491 × 3 = 10473 | 27 ×48 = 1296 | 1256 × 70 = 87920 |

Estimate the product.

| | | | | | |
|---|---|---|---|---|---|
| 13. | 46 × 3 = 150 | 98 × 7 = 700 | 234 × 9 = 1800 | 23 ×14 = 200 | 18 × 2 = 40 | 173 × 23 = 4000 |
| 14. | 432 × 53 = 20000 | 7832 × 24 = 160000 | 498 × 23 = 10000 | 87 ×49 = 4500 | 237 × 56 = 12000 | 132 × 78 = 8000 |

Spectrum Multiplication
Grade 4

Final Test
Chapters 1–4
78

**79**

Final Test Chapters 1–4

Multiply.

| | a | b | c | d | e | f |
|---|---|---|---|---|---|---|
| 15. | 81 × 9 = 729 | 23 × 4 = 92 | 63 × 7 = 441 | 22 × 3 = 66 | 78 × 9 = 702 | 94 × 3 = 282 |
| 16. | 90 × 8 = 720 | 36 × 5 = 180 | 52 × 3 = 156 | 44 × 2 = 88 | 73 × 5 = 365 | 87 × 8 = 696 |
| 17. | 465 × 3 = 1395 | 203 × 3 = 609 | 515 × 8 = 4120 | 150 × 3 = 450 | 8917 × 7 = 62419 | 711 × 6 = 4266 |
| 18. | 258 × 4 = 1032 | 6412 × 3 = 19236 | 330 × 3 = 990 | 703 × 6 = 4218 | 2900 × 9 = 26100 | 664 × 8 = 5312 |

Find the rule and complete the table.

19.

a

| In | Out |
|---|---|
| 1 | 10 |
| 2 | 18 |
| 3 | 26 |
| 4 | 34 |
| 5 | 42 |

multiply by 8 and add 2

b

| In | Out |
|---|---|
| 3 | 13 |
| 5 | 23 |
| 7 | 33 |
| 9 | 43 |
| 11 | 53 |

multiply by 5 and subtract 2

c

| In | Out |
|---|---|
| 1 | 13 |
| 4 | 43 |
| 7 | 73 |
| 8 | 83 |
| 10 | 103 |

multiply by 10 and add 3

Spectrum Multiplication
Grade 4

Final Test
Chapters 1–4
79

**80**

Final Test Chapters 1–4

Solve each problem. Show your work under each question.

20. Xavier loves to eat pears. He ate 2 a day for 48 days. How many pears did Xavier eat?

Xavier ate __96__ pears.

21. Clayton keeps pet mice. If his 33 mice have 12 babies each, how many mice will Clayton have in all?

Clayton will have __396__ mice.

22. In a tropical rain forest, the average annual rainfall is about 150 inches. After 5 years, about how much rain will have fallen in the rain forest?

About __750__ inches of rain will have fallen.

23. A class of 55 students went on a field trip to collect seashells. If the students collected 15 shells each, how many shells did they collect?

The students collected __825__ shells.

24. What is the next number in this pattern? Explain your answer.

3, 12, 57, 282, 1407 __7032; multiply each number by 5 and subtract 3__

Spectrum Multiplication
Grade 4

Final Test
Chapters 1–4
80

**81**

Final Test Chapters 1–4

Solve each problem. Show your work under each question.

25. Mrs. Rockwell checked on how much time her students spend doing homework. If all 23 students spend 20 hours each week, how much homework do the students do in a week?

They do __460__ hours of homework a week.

26. A cable program loans channel boxes to 21 community centers for a trial program. If there are 12 boxes for each center, how many boxes are being loaned?

There are __252__ boxes being loaned.

27. A girls' club is trying to get into the record books for the most hair braids. There are 372 girls. If each girl braids her hair into 40 little braids, how many braids will they have?

They will have __14880__ braids.

28. In one week, Pop sold ice cream cones to 2,375 people. If each customer had 2 scoops, how many scoops did Pop sell?

Pop sold __4750__ scoops of ice cream.

Spectrum Multiplication
Grade 4

Final Test
Chapters 1–4
81

**82**

Final Test Chapters 1–4

Solve each problem. Show your work under each question.

29. Students set up the chairs for the spring concert at Bethel High School. There were 25 rows with 10 chairs in each row. How many chairs did they set up?

They set up __250__ chairs.

30. The Ferris wheel at the fair gave 198 rides on opening day. If each ticket was good for 2 rides, how many tickets were used to ride the Ferris wheel? Write a multiplication equation to find how many tickets were used. Then, solve.

__2 x a = 198__

__99__ tickets were used to ride the Ferris wheel.

31. At the Bead Shop, there are 25 rows of glass beads. If there are 320 glass beads in each row, how many glass beads are in the shop?

There are __8000__ glass beads in the shop.

32. The cafeteria planned to bake 3 chocolate chip cookies for every student in the school. If there are 2,715 students, how many cookies does the cafeteria need to bake?

The cafeteria needs to bake __8145__ cookies.

Spectrum Multiplication
Grade 4

Final Test
Chapters 1–4
82

Spectrum Multiplication
Grade 4

Answer Key